D1065802

Dare to Choose Happy

Intuition, Clarity, Priority & Truth — Get What You Want with Grace and Ease

DARIENNE MOBLEY

KWE PUBLISHING

Mobley, Darienne. *Dare to Choose Happy: Intuition, Clarity, Priority & Truth—Get What You Want with Grace and Ease*

ISBN: 979-8-9878852-0-8

Library of Congress Control Number: 2023905490

Cover design by Michelle Fairbanks | Fresh Design https://freshdesignbooks.carbonmade.com/

KWE Publishing, www.kwepub.com

If you are interested in learning more about Darienne and her coaching programs, please visit https://darienneinc.com/ .

Sandra Storey Oliver

1937 – 1982

To my mother, who gave me in 22 short years what I would need to live the last 40+ without her.

TABLE OF CONTENTS

Acknowledgments

"All my roads have led me here." — *Collin Raye*

Life is a journey and mine has certainly made lots of twists and turns. I believe that we end up where we are supposed to be. But it would be impossible without the support of the people that were there for me along this road. Some of you drove the car when I didn't know how; some of you rode with me and navigated, some of you let me follow when I didn't know where I was headed; some of you followed me when I thought I did; and some of you stayed parked with me while I waited for the next part of the journey. All of you mattered. All of you made a difference. Even the difficult parts got me here.

First and foremost is my father, Dennis Oliver, and my sister Darla Davis. They have known me the longest and they have gone through all the ups and downs of my life. My father has been a strong support for me and a cheerleader. I remember when I went to college, he wrote me letters every week to let me know he was there. My sister and I have been through the battle of my mother's illness and passing. We have supported each other throughout our lives. She might say I became her mother that day in January 1982, but her love has carried me through all of my good and bad days.

There are too many family and friends to mention. Where do I start? My family is blended beautifully into this rich community that has accepted me into their lives and hearts. A special thank you to my stepmother, Ame, who added so much richness to our lives and stood in the gap for me. Just to name a few of my family: Oliver's, Davis', Duggin's, Wilhite's, Wilson's, Ladnier's, Mobley's and Bosse's. My life is richer because you are part of it.

My friends are the secret sauce of my happiness. Katie is first and foremost. We met in 1982 right after my mother passed and without asking for the job, she stepped up to be my friend, my mother when I needed it, my counselor and cohort. We have been through thick and thin together – literally and figuratively. To Jill, Chris, and Anne – you have been there to offer advice, laughter, encouragement, and support. There is nothing better than old friends. Friends that see you, know you and accept you. There are no words. There are so many friends not listed here. Thank you all.

My clients have allowed me into their lives. They have vulnerably trusted me with their successes and failures. More importantly, they let me see their fears and feelings of inadequacy. My deepest gratitude goes to them. This career that I am so blessed to be able to do is because of them.

Kim Eley, KWE Publishing, and her team are the reason there is a book to read. I met Kim at a women's retreat. She made writing and publishing a book sound possible. Without her support, encouragement, editing and polite suggestions I would not be here.

To all of you who said – "you should write a book", even though I laughed on the outside, you planted a seed. Thank you. Here it is.

Dan Mobley is my daily reminder that I am loved. Hope he feels that way too. He makes sure there is gas in my car, coffee in the morning and has read every page of this self-help book. Not his genre of reading! He and I married eighteen years ago, and my life is better because of him. The best thing I can say is that he makes me feel safe.

And last, is my daughter, Storey. She is everything. She is smart, funny, sensitive, and beautiful. She is talented and wise. No one can call me out on my stuff like she can. I am proud of the woman she has become. What I am sure of is that when my life is over, I leave something good behind.

How to Approach this Book

I believe you have what you need to live your best life right now. I believe you are enough today. I also believe that most of us don't know how to slow down enough and which questions to ask to get clear so that you can live with intention and purpose. I created this book to hold space for you to slow down and ask these important questions. My intention is to share what I have learned about myself and other women that hopefully is relevant to your life and to provide the framework for you to stop and examine what is working and what might need tweaking. Sometimes, it is just small changes that have a big impact.

I also know that this book is one in a sea of personal development options for you. Having always been drawn to the 'how to be better' aisle, I have learned from books that taught me something new. Maybe that is true for you too. Thank you for choosing this one.

This entire book—*Dare to Choose Happy*—is based on the premise that we get to choose. We get to slow down, take a breath, and relax. We get to see situations differently. We get to decide what success looks like for us. We can choose happy for ourselves.

It is not necessary to start on the first page and end on the last and do every exercise in this book. This is not a goal to be reached. A task to be checked off. This is for your enjoyment and growth. I believe that your intuition will guide you to the section of this book that is most important for you to start. Just trust your gut. I hope you laugh, see yourself in my stories and find some nuggets that will make your life just a little better. Don't do every exercise. There is not an award for those that do, I promise. Choose the exercises that make sense or inspire you in some way. You get to decide how to use this book.

My wish is that lots of people buy this book. Nobody says that out loud, but it is true. But for me, it is more important that you find something useful in this book. I want it to find a permanent place on your bedside table. I want you to turn down pages and highlight sections that you want to remember. I want you to pull this book out every year and either redo exercises that you have already done or try some you didn't do last year.

As written in the *Velveteen Rabbit* – I want this book to be real to you. Used, beaten up and marked up. Because when you are real you can't be ugly, except to people who don't understand. May this book be real to you.

Enjoy!

—Darienne

Dare to Choose Happy

Why Me? Why This Book?

Happiness—when you feel satisfied and fulfilled.
Happiness is a feeling of contentment, that life is just as
it should be.

I have been dancing as fast as I can for most of my life trying to make you like me. I became what I thought you wanted me to be. Doing me didn't seem like enough. I would surely disappoint others if they knew me. I believed that having the approval of others (always fickle) was the most important barometer of my wellbeing.

Finding my voice and speaking my truth have been the lessons that I needed to learn in this life. I am still finding out what choosing happy is for me – and thought maybe you could learn from my experiences on how to choose you and your own happy.

Once I decided to show up as myself, life was easier. Understanding that others' opinions of me were not as important as my opinion of myself was the first step. Dr. Phil says, "We would not worry so much about what others think of us if we knew how little they did."

Does this sound familiar?

I am strong, confident, and successful. I'm also weak, insecure, and a failure. Both statements are true. And I bet they are for you too. What I've done in my life is to try to live somewhere in the middle, in that sweet spot between strong and weak. If I'm too strong, then that gets perceived as bitchy; if I'm too weak, then that gets seen as pitiful.

By trying to avoid going too far toward one end of the spectrum or the other, I've lived small, having made decisions that kept me from being visible and stepping into my light. I know I don't want to do that anymore. Do you?

I work with professional women who are smart, confident, and successful on the outside, but who feel deep fears and insecurity on the inside. They question their decisions and constantly beat themselves up with the 'should' – "I should be a better mother;" "I should have gone to that meeting;" "I should have worked harder," and "I should have cooked dinner every night." That constant barrage of negative self-talk keeps them from stepping into their light too. Does that happen for you?

My life's work is to help you create the best version of yourself on the outside, but more importantly on the inside.

I have had a successful career by others' standards. Big jobs, big responsibilities, and a feeling of imposter syndrome most of the time. I know the exhausted feeling of coming home from a long, stressful day at work to start the home work that needed to be done. Why we believe that getting help would result in failure is beyond me now. I remember being in a meeting with the Governor of Mississippi during the day and ending it sitting in a circle with my daughter at her Brownie meeting. The irony of that has stayed with me. But that is what makes up our lives.

We have been taught that we eat last. Everyone must be fed, taken care of, and then we can relax. I believe that is so wrong.

Empty Cup Syndrome

We can't give from an empty cup. We have all heard the airline stewardess announce that in times of disaster to put your own mask on first. But only when the plane is going down. I want to choose happy on clear days when the flight is good. I want to put me first sometimes.

I had a client that was exhausted and run down physically and mentally. I explained that she had to put herself first. She became upset and told me that her mother had taught her that God came first, family next, and then her.

Everyone else's needs came before hers. She also said that her faith was that it would be selfish to take care of herself. My guess is that she is still exhausted. I don't believe that God wants us to be exhausted and running on empty. He wants us to be fulfilled and happy. Choosing happy is brave and scary, but I can help you do it.

Happy Has Been Underrated

Even when I was picking the title of this book and shared it with others, some said that happy was not serious enough, and it sounded like a light book. Happy makes us uncomfortable because we don't really know how to be happy, and we certainly can't choose happy if it makes anyone else uncomfortable. We must be hard-working, move up in our careers, be successful. Happy almost seems silly. Not meaningful. No time for that.

I don't remember when I was younger and offered jobs, if I ever asked – will that job make me happy? My questions were more around the salary, the staff, upward mobility and if others would perceive it as a move up. I have been impressed with millennials that have said to me, "I am not happy. My job doesn't make me happy." I have a friend whose son was working in a big city for a reputable company – successful – right out of college. Recently, he called his parents and said, "I am not happy." He then moved across the country for a job that spoke to him. He chose happy. And I see that as brave.

90 Words A Minute

To tell you who I am, this story is it. It is not just that I had this big career. Or that hundreds of professional women have chosen me to be their life and leadership coach. No, the story that sums me up happened in 1981 in Gulfport, Mississippi.

I graduated from college with a degree in Speech Communication. I remember going to my advisor and asking what kind of job I should be looking for. My father had questioned my major many times, always asking

– "What are you going to do?" My advisor mentioned journalism, teaching, or sales and catering in a hotel. I chose door number three. I moved back home to the Gulf Coast and started getting in touch with the hotels. None of them would hire me. I had a degree, a little personality, and not much else.

After about six weeks, I went to an employment agency. Some of you reading this don't even know what an employment agency is – think Google or Indeed. I found myself walking into a bank in downtown Gulfport, Mississippi, waiting for Wayne Grant, the Vice President. He would be the person that I needed most but I had no idea. The job was Student Loan Coordinator and his secretary. I had no idea what either of those titles meant but I really needed a job.

Wayne was stern; I was nervous. He intimidated me with his questions. My DISCTM assessment is an "I" which means that making you like me is my go-to. We can get through lots of mistakes if you like me. Well, there was certainly no outward indication that Wayne liked me.

Then he asked me the now famous question. "How fast do you type?" I paused and looked Wayne right in the eye and said with confidence – "90 words a minute."

The truth is that I never took typing (I know how crazy that seems now). I did not know what a good answer would be, so hence 90. I saw Wayne's eyes light up for the first time and I knew I was in trouble. I got the job. I bought myself a typing-for-dummies type of book. I thought I would be in an office and could figure this out.

On the first day, I dressed up to start my new job. I was nervous. My desk was in the lobby of the bank. There was no room to hide. The phone rang and someone said it was for me. When I asked which line (I had never worked in a big office before), she seemed surprised and answered, "the one that's lit up." It took about three weeks for Wayne to call me into his office. I thought I knew what was coming. It was clear at this point that he had figured out my big lie. I kept listening for the "you are fired." Instead, he said that the bank wanted to pay to send me to typing school. I was shocked and relieved.

Wayne gave me a skill I would need for the rest of my life. He did the most kind and thoughtful thing that anyone has ever done for me. I often ask myself, "Who can I be Wayne Grant to?"

When I walked into the Natchez Eola Hotel interviewing for a sales position (my dream job), the sales director asked me the same question. "How fast do you type?" I was ready. I had even brought my certificate. I would not have gotten that job if not for Wayne.

So, what does this say about me? I sometimes do brave things. I have a belief that most things will work out. And I make shit up!

In this book, I share my own experiences, the funny ones, and the sad ones. I share my own vulnerability and mistakes that I have made. I share the process that I went through and now use with my clients helping them to choose happy.

What would be different for you if you put your toe in the water of putting your oxygen mask on – filling up your cup? My guess is that if you were filled up, you would be better in all the areas of your life. It is time to unpack those buckets (as I call them) and see which ones are serving you and which ones you can let go. The first step is in making the commitment to read the book and do the exercises. Choose happy!

Choose Happy Matters

Happy is a feeling we might have on an occasional day or during a particularly meaningful event. Do you feel happy on vacation? Did you feel happy on your wedding day? Did you feel happy when you got the promotion? Or the new house? What if you felt happy on a random Tuesday?

I believed that happy just happened. On vacation, I was usually so busy making sure that everyone else was happy – that I didn't focus on my own happiness. So maybe, there would be a moment on vacation when there was peace and for that moment, I felt happy. Usually, I didn't stop to notice it.

We choose happy – we choose perspective, and we choose how we show up and respond to others in our lives. For most of my life, I blamed others for what was not working. Bosses, husbands, clients, or family. Looking back, I can clearly see that I was the one that didn't choose me and therefore, didn't choose happy. For me, I usually didn't even ask for what I knew in my gut would make the happy. I wish I had made more noise. Understood that my happiness was a priority. Believing that I matter enough to be honest is a hard-earned lesson.

I love the song "How You Live (Turn Up the Music)" by Point of Grace. If you scan this QR code, it will take you to the YouTube video for this wonderful song.

For me, I had some defining happy moments. Those times when I went against what others thought was best for me and chose me. Chose to trust my intuition.

I was married when I was twenty-two to a nice man that I had dated through college. I wasn't in love with him but could never have said that out loud. My mother was dying of pancreatic cancer and here was someone that said he would be there for me. My fear of being alone was greater than my ability to know that the marriage was not right. After two years, I knew. I knew that I did not have what other happy couples had. There was a spark, a connectedness in them that I was lacking. My parents weren't on board with my choosing to end that marriage. I bravely chose me. Against all the noise and feeling of failure and disappointing of others. I am sorry that I chose my first husband for all the wrong reasons. That is my failure. Yet, looking back, I am proud that I chose happy in the end. I chose me bravely.

I was twenty-five and looking for a job. I was offered a job with an ad agency. The money was good, and it would look like a move-up for me. My other offer was from a woman, Kathy Jackson, who owned an association management company. I had been working there part-time for a few months while I was looking for the next big ride. I liked Kathy. I felt comfortable working with her. She could not offer me the same money. My friends and family thought that was reason enough to take the other job. I knew in my gut that Kathy was someone that I wanted to work with. By choosing happy and not money or title, I made the right choice. In about a year, I bought 50% of Kathy's company, Mississippi Association Managers, and we managed that business for over 10 years together. The friendship was vital to my happiness and the work was important to my professional growth. A choosing happy moment for sure.

What I see is that when I chose me over what others would have chosen for me, I have chosen happy. It is hard to disappoint others. In the end, my family and friends just wanted me to be happy. They only offered their opinion. It was me that many times valued their opinion over my own.

You want to be happy. Of that I am confident. For some of you, you just don't know how to start. How to speak up. How to be loud. How to be messy. I get it. But it is time. Choosing happy is mandatory for living your best life so you can have fulfillment, confidence, and contentment.

Exercises

Date (If you are like me, you have these books and re-read them later and wonder when you wrote them?)

_____

What are you hoping to get out of this book?

_____

_____

_____

Why did you pick it up?

_____

_____

What is one change that would have the greatest impact on your happiness? Don't overthink this –

_____

_____

"Some say life begins at 40. Others at 50. All nonsense! Life begins when we decide to stop pleasing the audience." A Simple View—Lynette Evans

Intentional Action Pillars

Acting by design to create a desired future

We are busy. Our heads are down doing the list. Getting through the inbox and checking off the tasks. That was true for me. Winning was getting it all done. When people asked how I was, my go-to was, "I am so busy." Somehow busy became a synonym for successful. Was I making intentional decisions? Who knew what that even meant? Not me.

In 2006 I had resigned from the Louisiana Office of Tourism. I was the Assistant Secretary (the boss of tourism for the state). While that was a big job, a respected job – I wasn't happy. I could do the job, but it wasn't aligned with my gifts and talents. While I did a good job of convincing others that I was successful and effective, I knew I wasn't. And I quit. Talk about choosing happy. I gave up insurance, retirement and – oh yeah – the salary. Bigger than that, I gave up the title – which seemed more important than all the other stuff. I had no idea what I would do. I had no idea what I was good at.

I thought about starting my own company. What services could I offer? What would others pay me to do? Darienne Inc. was born. The name of my company is not from a place of conceit. It was the only element of this new business I was sure about.

I started out doing tourism consulting. That was my area of expertise. I had worked in the tourism industry for over 25 years at that point.

Somewhere around 2012, I hired a coach. I didn't really understand what they did. I asked myself in the middle of the night, "Is this it, God? I know you have given me so much, but is there more?" I believed that I was selfish for asking. I had the stuff: a good marriage, a successful business, a beautiful daughter, and good friends. If you have all of that, well, shouldn't you be happy?

My coach asked me hard questions. What are you good at? What lights you up? Where do you want to live? And with whom? I didn't have answers for any of those questions. I was ready to find out. Through three years of digging deep, I was able to write my vision for my life.

"I live by water. I do work that uses my gifts and talents and I am connected to my family, friends, and community." —Darienne Mobley

At the time I wrote this vision, I did not live by water. I did not use my gifts in my job. I felt very lonely and disconnected. It took digging deep, asking myself hard questions, and having difficult conversations. It took me choosing happy. I now live in Ocean Springs, Mississippi, on the Gulf of Mexico. I am good at coaching, speaking, training, and hopefully writing. There is an ease to my work and life these days. It is now 2023 and that vision is my life.

If I could speak up for me, you can too.

The Pillars

When I was working with my coach, she walked me through a process to get clear about what I wanted. I would not be called selfless by my friends. And yet, my actions were making sure that everyone in my orbit was okay. I needed to not make waves or be trouble. I had no opinions on anything. I am sure I came across as weak and wimpy. What most of my clients want is help with how to be less busy; how to find time for themselves; how to reduce the stress and anxiety in their lives and how to be healthier.

What I have developed is a strategy or a process for getting what you want with grace and ease. It is called *Intentional Action*. That means being intentional about how you show up in your day, what you choose to focus on, and how you define success. This process has transformed many of my clients who say they feel more peace, confidence, and calm in their day. They feel lighter and more at ease.

The Intentional Action Pillars are Intuition, Clarity, Priority, and Truth. Each of these is important. Many of my clients want to jump in at Priority – they want to know how to get the most stuff done! But, without intuition and clarity, they flounder and fall back on their old habits. I will walk you through each pillar in this book and guide you through the process. You will have a vision of what matters most and the strategies to get there.

Intuition

Intuition is this gift from God that is in all of us. It is that quiet voice that speaks to us and I believe it is always leading us to the "next right thing." But most of us are so busy and our lives are so full of noise that we don't hear it. Have you ever had a problem or an important decision to make and you go to all of your friends asking for advice? They each give you their best answer and then you are more confused because your friends did not all agree. Then you must decipher through all their opinions and still don't know what your opinion is. It is like Dorothy from the Wizard of Oz; you always had it – you always had intuition and your truth. Learn how to listen and trust that voice that is always leading you to the best decisions.

Clarity

Clarity is this missing piece for most of us. We don't have a vision. We are just trying to get today done. We want to get to the end of the day and not get in trouble, or to not have forgotten some important meeting or project, and still have enough energy to fix dinner and take care of our at-home responsibilities. Most of you—like I used to be — fall into a chair after all that and get lost in some television show to decompress. We are busy. We wear busy like a badge. We must be ok if we are busy. We get very comfortable with that anxiety of "I can't get all this done." I believe there is a better way. The first step is to decide for yourself (not your spouse or children or friends) what you want. Getting clear about what is important to you frees up all the fuzziness and allows you to focus on that. Focus on what would make your life better – more meaningful. Making sure the busy makes sense.

A vision for your life feels big. But, writing down what you want to be or do or have seems doable—or at least it does to my clients.

Priority

So, intuition and clarity are about "why" and "what" in your life. Priority is about the "how." Now, you are ready to dig into my top tips for being more productive.

The most important element of priority is that you decide what your day is going to look like. You look at your calendar and tasks and decide what to focus on. You set up your day to get the most important things done. For many of you, I know that you think that you don't get to decide – that others decide for you with their interruptions, their emergencies, and all the other distractions. But I believe that you get to decide more than you think. How you use that uninterrupted time is up to you.

Also, in prioritizing it is vital to learn how to say "No" with grace and kindness. It is knowing which buckets to release. Saying "No" is the keystone of taking back control of your life. We say "Yes" for tons of reasons that usually have nothing to do with what we want to do but everything to do with pleasing others. Think before you say "Yes" – next time.

Truth

Now, you are ready to tackle speaking your truth. Most of us don't like to have difficult conversations. It is easier to just go along. It is no big deal, right?

Maybe not. Speaking up about the easy things is a good place to start. Speaking up gets easier. It is like a muscle we use in exercise. The more we do it, the easier it becomes. Learn how to speak up from a place of honesty and not anger. It will change your life.

Hope is the voice that meets you in the storm and says there is more than we can see right now.

Intuition – Use Your Inside Voice

Intuition – the ability to understand something immediately without the need for conscious reasoning.

We all have it – that voice in our gut that says, "Don't take that job," "Don't have that 3rd glass of wine" or "Yes, you can do that." Often, we don't listen to that voice. We look outside of ourselves to find the answers. Using outside resources is helpful and can help you fine-tune your intuition. That can be found in coaching, therapy, books and podcasts, as well as advice from others. Ultimately, your intuition is the best source. You know what you want, what is standing in the way, who is draining you of oxygen, and who is holding you back. You know when your life is running on empty and when it is full and alive.

So, if we know, why don't we listen? Why don't we use our inside voice more? We don't listen for several reasons. We don't really want to know. We don't trust ourselves. We don't want to make the changes that would be needed if we listened and acted on that intuition.

I have always been aware of my intuition. That quiet voice that said, "Don't marry that guy," "Don't take that job." I also understood that it was God's voice. It was always leading to the next right thing. I heard that voice but acting on it was hard. That meant blowing up my life at times and letting others down. My intuition about my decisions was not what others thought was right for me. I usually chose what would keep me in their good graces.

I don't have many regrets. I like to see the bad stuff as lessons. And there has been some bad stuff. As hard as it is to say, most of the bad things were created by me. I have been married three times. Once for two years, once for fifteen and the current one for seventeen. I am not proud. I am not bragging. I have failed. One of my dreams for my daughter was that she would not be from a broken home. I was from a broken home and hoped to spare her. Husband #1 was unfortunately an avoidable mistake. I wish I had been more aware and had the ability to speak up. I didn't.

Husband #2 is a good man. I was deeply in love with him. We had a happy marriage for a long time. What brings me peace is knowing that he is happier in his current marriage to a fabulous partner.

We have this unique friendship now and have both raised our daughter in the best way possible. What I can see as the blessing of that marriage is Storey Kate, our daughter. He has been the best father to her. Even when

I explained that I had a job opportunity in Baton Rouge, Louisiana, and he lived in Jackson, Mississippi, he said we would make it work. And, we did.

What I had to realize was that the common denominator in those two failed marriages was me. It wasn't them. I never let them see me. I believed I wasn't good enough deep down. I became what I thought they wanted me to be for as long as I could. I wasn't emotionally available. I let "me" down. And them.

Husband #3 is my destination relationship. I got it right. I am taken care of, safe, protected and loved. I hope I do those things for him. We are as different as we can be. Creamy and crunchy is how we describe ourselves (you know – peanut butter). I was single for six years before we met and those were the most important years of my personal growth. I worked hard to take accountability for my actions. I was ready when he came along. He is a caring man who loves deeply. If he is in your corner, he never waivers. He will take up for you no matter what.

We had a lot to blend. At the time we married, he had two children and four grandchildren. Two grandchildren came later. He took on the day-to-day step-parenting for my twelve-year-old daughter. He has treated Storey like a daughter since the beginning. I love all of the family members that make up our blended lives.

I remember when he came to my parents' house for Thanksgiving for the first time. My stepmother took me aside and asked, "Do we put him in the pictures?" She was asking if he would be around next year. She was thinking, *why waste a good family picture if we could avoid it?* I told her to include him. I was right. I am glad that I knew he would be back because I can't imagine saying, "Hey, can you stay out of our pictures?"

Quiet Time Is Mandatory

The best way to get inside your body and out of your head is getting quiet. That means changing something in your routine to clear your head. For my clients, they get that this is helpful, but they are busy, and this feels like a waste of time when they could be getting something more important done. Sound familiar? Once again taking themselves off the list because "there simply isn't enough time."

What is this magical quiet time? You decide when, where and what it is for you. All that is required is a quiet space, no dinging notifications or television sounds to distract you. You can call it prayer, meditation, or centering. You can sit on your back patio, favorite chair or in bed. The time it takes to get quiet is five minutes. More if you can. Even set an alarm if you want. I get asked, "Doesn't your mind wander?" Of course, it does. In the beginning, you start going through your calendar, your tasks and even your grocery list. You acknowledge those thoughts and then let them go.

For me, it looks like this:

Taking several deep breaths.

Tuning into my physical body, noting pain or discomfort.
I note anything that comes up.

Often, we don't pay attention to cues that our body is sending us.

Asking myself four questions:

What do I need to focus on today? (usually a work thing)

What do I need today? (usually a personal thing)

What am I grateful for?

How do I feel today?

That's it. Nothing too woo-woo. Just a centering exercise that changes your day and then your life. Why? Because for five minutes you are aware of what you need – where you can find your oxygen.

When I do this exercise, I feel calmer, more at peace and ready to step into my day. My energy is different. My reaction to problems is different. I am more available to the people in my world. For leaders, this allows you to get out of your own way and be more available to your team.

Living Out Loud

There have been many times that I have taken risks that looking back do not seem to fit who I am. I am shy and insecure. I have lived with anxiety that I was not enough for so long, that I do not even recognize the voice in my head anymore. Choosing happy is big and brave and stepping outside of ourselves. Choosing happy is living out loud.

So, the risk-taking moments are those moments when I did something scary. Doing that thing that feels too big and jumping in anyway.

My Living Out Loud Moments

Since I was a freshman in high school, I wanted to be in the Junior Miss Pageant. I had never been in a beauty pageant, and no one had ever suggested I should. During my senior year of high school, I went to my mother and asked her if I could do it. She paused, looking down reading the material and then asked, "Don't these girls have talent?" in her kindest, most loving voice. When I said "Yes," I don't think she felt better. She then asked, "What is yours?" I explained that I was going to do a comedy routine. I still don't think she felt better. My parents wore sunglasses and sat in the back row. Not really, but that makes the story better. I remember it as the scariest thing I had done. I did not win Junior Miss. I did win the scholastic award and Miss Congeniality. Winning was never the goal but showing up was. I remember feeling so proud. I chose happy.

In 2000, a new governor was elected in Mississippi. I was the Director of the Mississippi Tourism Association, the private sector association of tourism statewide. In December of 1999, a close friend called and told me to close the door to my office. He went on to say that the industry should be proactive in recommending a candidate to the governor for the position of Director of Tourism. I asked him, "Who should we recommend?" and he said, "You." I was silent. I was putting up road blocks in my mind about why I was not the right person for the job. Finally, I said, "A lot of people don't like the Director of Tourism, I don't know if I can handle all that criticism." He immediately said, "What rock do you live under? Most people don't like you now!" He did not get me that job. He opened my mind up to consider it. Choosing happy in that situation was the bravest thing I have ever done. I asked an executive at the Mississippi Development Authority to "Pick Me." I couldn't breathe and almost ran from his office. Three weeks later, I received the call that said I would be the Director of Tourism for the State. That living out loud moment changed the trajectory of my career and life.

What I know is that the times that I have overridden the fear, my life has always landed in a better place. I am so glad that the "just do it voice" was louder than the "I can't do it" one.

Looking Back – Looking Forward

I like to take some time in the craziness of December to first look back over the past year and then look forward to the new year.

This pause gives me perspective and appreciation for what was accomplished instead of focusing on what I didn't get done. My practice is easy. It is called mind mapping. There are dozens of examples online. The purpose of mind mapping is to provide a structured way to capture and organize ideas and information. The technique helps users to understand concepts by breaking them down into their component parts. It is used to develop new ideas, or to break down and better understand existing information.

Upcoming Year - I start with a sheet of paper and some colored pencils. I draw a tree with branches. On the tree trunk, I write in the current year. On the branches, I write in the roles in my life (work, home, family, self, friends). Next, I add in other aspects of my life like fun, spiritual, relationships, or anything that bubbles up for me.

Now, the fun part – I start adding leaves and writing in the leaves the things I want to do in those areas of my life. Like, under personal—I might put exercise consistently, get monthly massages, spend time with friends, lose weight, or meditate regularly.

Keep your mind mapping tree in a place where you can review it periodically. I suggest that monthly you take about 20-30 minutes, review the dream tree, and write down action steps that month that will make those dreams come true.

There aren't dream leaves that are too silly or too much about stuff. If you really want a certain car—write it down. If you want to make a certain amount of money—write it down. If you want a certain house—write it down. Don't censor your dreams because they are too big.

For me, I have found power in manifesting what I want by writing it down on paper. The act solidifies it in my brain and starts to make it happen. Let's be honest—I don't get everything on the dream tree each year, but I believe I get more of it than if I did not write it down. This is the act of appreciation. Appreciating the things that do happen, the moments of peace and laughter that I did have and the moments that I did choose happy.

Enough is Enough

We all have a voice inside of us that says, "I am not ___ enough." Fill in the blank. I am not good enough, smart enough, pretty enough, happy enough. Even happy is on the list. For me, I am not good enough has resonated through me for as long as I can remember. That voice has kept me from trying things. From instigating relationships. From speaking up. What I had to say couldn't be smart enough to matter.

In choosing happy, we can't ignore the voice and pretend it isn't there. We must acknowledge it, hear it, and then question it. Is it true? In my thirties the voice was too loud to ignore. Today, I can hear it, ask if that is true, and most often the answer is that I am enough. Accepting that I have things I am good at and things I suck at is vital to accepting myself. The bottom line is that I am good enough and so are you.

That voice kept me from doing things that would allow others to see the truth that I was not enough. I regret the things I never tried because I thought I would fail.

I have never ridden a horse.

I have never snow skied.

I have never played sports.

I have never gone to an exercise class that might be too hard.

I have never tried anything that was scary.

Spirit and Ego – The Dance

Inside of us we have both—the ego and the spirit. Our ego is there to propel us forward. The ego says get ahead. Succeed. Win. It is our masculine energy. And we need it.

The spirit energy is our feminine energy, and it says, *just be yourself, relax, be kind and compassionate.* Our spirit energy has been seen in the past as negative.

When I was younger, we were taught that to be recognized, we needed to dress in a more masculine way to fit in. We wore suits and basic colors. It is crazy to think about that today. The message was that too girly was not okay. Being us was not okay. And the truth is that it has been proven that feminine characteristics and strengths are what business needs today. Compassion, grace, cooperation, and collaboration are just a few of the traits that matter in today's workplace.

I have always been more connected with my ego. I had a chaotic childhood, and I think I turned off the feelings button. It was easier to not feel. My safe place was school. I excelled. I understood the rules. I made good grades and was recognized for that. I succeeded.

In work, ego energy is seen as the powerful way to operate. Now, we know that our spirit energy of empathy, cooperation, team building and openness all matter today in companies. We don't need to hide either. We need both to live a balanced life.

What is feminine energy? In *Happier Human* by Sarah Kristenson, she states that feminine energy is all the nurturing traits it takes to connect to human beings in a meaningful and fulfilling way. It is being compassionate, kind, empathetic, patient, and emotional. It is about embracing your intuition and creativity.

Vulnerability – The Key to Connection and Intimacy

Every client I have cringes when I mention vulnerability. Too much! Too exposed! We all crave intimacy, connectedness and to be seen. But the way to those things is through letting people see you – being vulnerable. This doesn't mean throwing up all your past issues with anyone that walks by. It does mean letting those that you trust know you. Really know you. Not just the pretty stuff. Not just the happy stuff. Vulnerability is saying "I love you" first. "I am scared. I don't have it all together. I need help."

Vulnerability has been called the snowball effect. If I have the courage to be vulnerable with you, you will in effect be vulnerable with me. I think back on my friendships. If asked, "How are you?" my answer was "Fine." I went through a divorce and navigated being a single mother with a demanding career. I felt overwhelmed most of the time. I never admitted that. I wonder what they might have shared with me if I wasn't so determined to keep up my armor. What I know is that our friendships were not as deep as they could have been if I had had the guts to let my veil down.

In my job, there were staff meetings on Monday mornings at 7:30 AM. I had a six-year-old daughter. I was the only woman on the executive team with a young child. Mentioning that I had to get my child to school would have felt like I wasn't up to the job. You can't drop a child off at school at 7 AM. There is no one there. When my friends offered to help, I declined. Never did I want to be the cause of anyone going out of their way for me. And so, I hired babysitters to help. I could pay someone but not accept kindness. Looking back this makes me sad.

No one talks about vulnerability better than Brené Brown. This quote resonated with me, and I hope it does for you.

"Vulnerability is the core of shame and fear and our struggle for worthiness, but it appears that it's also the birthplace of joy, of creativity, of belonging, of love."
—Brené Brown

Trusting others is the vital key to allowing ourselves to be real, to be honest, and to open up about what is going on behind the veil. To be connected, we must let the veil down a little and let others in. Our fear is that they will see our weakness. We believe they will judge, criticize, and reject us. And we declare the way to keep ourselves safe is to never let them see us sweat. The opposite is true.

My clients often say, "I can do vulnerability at home, but it is weak to be vulnerable at work. I need my employees to see me as confident and strong." Is that true? Wouldn't your employees trust and respect you more if you let them see you? If you let your guard down, let down the "I have it all together" face, couldn't they then see you as human and just like them? Wouldn't that allow for a stronger team?

How do you do it?

In *Today's Leaders Need Vulnerability, Not Bravado* by Amy C. Edmondson and Thomas Chamorro-Premuzic, they discuss the value of being vulnerable at work. They stated:

> "People in organizations of all types are better off when their leaders are smart, honest, and caring when taking bold, potentially unpopular actions — when their focus is on helping the organization move forward, not on how they look and certainly not on creating a <u>false sense of invincibility</u> that actually harms people.

> In a complex and uncertain world that demands constant <u>learning and agility,</u> the most apt and adaptable leaders are those who are aware of their limitations, have the necessary humility to grow their own and others' potential, and are courageous and curious enough to create sincere and open connections with others. They build inclusive team climates with <u>psychological safety</u> that foster constructive criticism and dissent.

Above all, they embrace truth: They are more interested in understanding reality than in being right and are not afraid to accept that they were wrong. This allows them to welcome criticism — not because they like it any more than the rest of us, but because they know it's necessary to make progress. Altogether, this is a very different type than the macho-style leader who is rarely right yet seldom in doubt."

And then when sharing how people can make changes in their leadership style, they make these suggestions:

Start by telling the truth.

Ask for help.

Go outside of your comfort zone.

When you make a mistake, admit it, and apologize.

Engage others in your journey of self-improvement.

Gratitude is the Key

There is a misperception that happy people are grateful. The opposite is true. Grateful people are happy. When we focus on what is right, what is working – we see things differently. I believe what we focus on expands. When we focus on the bad parts, we see more bad parts. When we focus on the good stuff, we see more of that. It is a law of the universe. I have been practicing gratitude since I heard Oprah talk about it years ago. Every morning, I look around to recognize my blessings. Sometimes, the list is the same as yesterday. I am always surprised by how blessed I have been. I am sure you have been too. We just need to recognize and appreciate it.

I don't want to leave you with this sense that my life is easy or that I never have sadness or anger. Or that others haven't disappointed me. All of the above is true. This past year, I have had some health issues that have caused me pain and anxiety. So a grateful practice does not take away the yucky stuff, it just allows me to see a ray of sunshine even in the pain.

Numbing is Not the Cure

We all do it. We all numb our feelings in one way or the other. Some of us more than others. We may use overeating, drinking, shopping, or watching television. None of these are bad. They only become negative actions in our life if our primary objective is to shut off the "feeling valve." I heard an expert say that we can't numb the pain without numbing the joy. That was the first time that I realized that living in the middle by blocking bad feelings was also blocking the good ones. That was the beginning of a journey for me to be aware of how I numbed and asked myself the question, "Does that still work for me and am I ready to change?"

My primary numbing behavior has always been food. From a young age, I went to the refrigerator and took a bite out of the leftovers – cold. I needed soothing and I wasn't getting it. Those cold bites of food did it for me. So, my weight and relationship with food has been part of my life journey. For years, I realized that when I came home from school, I got a snack. Many years later, I saw that same pattern repeating itself. When I came home from work – I got a snack. Some of that were habits which are hard to break. The other part of that was my brain wanting that feeling of being safe and familiar.

My secret numbing behavior has been drinking. My friends and family never thought I had a problem with alcohol. I knew I did. My intuition knew. When I started, I did not stop—sometimes. Enough times that I knew it was a problem. I had hundreds of mornings when I had no idea what I had done or said and wondered what others thought of me. Did they know? I hid my embarrassment and my hangovers. For me, it was validation that I wasn't good enough.

Over my life, I had made promises about moderating my behavior, which never worked. I quit several times and then decided it wasn't a problem and went back to drinking. I made the decision to quit drinking altogether in 2021. As of this writing, I have been alcohol free for 16 months. I know that of all the changes I have made in my life to live my best life, this was the most important and the hardest.

There was a night in August 2021 when we were having drinks with our neighbors and friends. I was enjoying the night and downing my wine. I realized the next morning that I had about a bottle and a half of red wine. I was embarrassed and ashamed.

Shame lives in the dark. Speaking up about my drinking is both vulnerable and true and takes the shame out of it. After a few months, I shared this with my family and friends. I remember one of the hardest times was a beach trip with my best friends. I had been alcohol free for a month. They knew me as the wine drinker. When you stop drinking it affects others. They feel badly if they drink. They want us to be what we have always been and are a little uncomfortable with the new version. I didn't want to talk about it yet since I wasn't sure I would stick to my plan. But I knew that if I didn't talk about it – it would be easier to slip up. So, I shared my truth, and they loved me through it. They all said that they loved me drinking or not drinking. They have been a huge source of support and love.

The other lesson about my drinking or not drinking was that most people didn't care. It wasn't about them nor did it affect them.

What I realized when I stopped drinking is that I suffered from anxiety. I wasn't reaching for a glass of wine, so I was faced with feelings that I had buried, memories that I chose to pack up and the anxiety of all the things that could go wrong.

One time I was on a trip with my daughter. We had ordered an Uber to pick us up at 6 AM to go to the airport. I was up all night thinking about all the things that could go wrong. What if Uber didn't show up? What if we missed our flight? It was then that I realized that these feelings and thoughts were anxiety. I called my doctor when I got home. I explained what was going on. His answer was that alcohol was the liquid Zoloft. I went on anxiety meds and went into therapy. Both have been vital to my mental health.

For me, abstaining is much easier than moderating. I wish I was able to have two glasses of wine. I can't. My intuition was yelling at me that this was a problem and I ignored that for many years. I also realized how much head space the drinking thoughts were taking up. "Will I drink today? How much will I drink? Will I stop? Will I feel bad tomorrow?" My quitting alcohol was choosing happy. No one ever said choosing happy was easy.

Success – What is Your Definition?

For me, success was always about the title. It was about the accomplishment. It was about how many people I managed or how big my budget was—whatever it was that I thought other people would be impressed by. It was completely in the hands of others. I felt successful when others told me I was. It's our ego that drives us to label success that way.

That spirit side of us knows that real success is: Are we happy? Are we fulfilled? Do we feel connected and seen? Do we feel loved? Does our life matter?

What I'm starting to realize is that success is about how I feel. I feel abundant these days. Abundant in relationships, opportunity, and work.

Stephen R. Covey talks about success in his book, *Seven Habits of Highly Effective People.* The chapter is called, "Begin with the End in Mind." This is what he says.

"To begin with the end in mind means to start with a clear understanding of your destination. It means to know where you're going so that you better understand where you are now and so that the steps you take are always in the right direction."

Exercise

Quiet Time

Find a place in your home or office that you can shut down the noise for five minutes. Sit quietly, close your eyes, and breathe. Take three breaths and then ask yourself these three questions.

What is my focus today?

What do I need today?

What am I grateful for?

Living Out Loud

What are your living out loud moments?

_____

_____

_____

_____

Which living out loud moments changed your life? How?

_____

_____

_____

_____

What regrets do you have for the times that you could have but didn't live out loud?

_____

_____

_____

_____

Spirit and Ego Exercise

Get quiet for a few minutes and then just write whatever comes up to answer this question. Don't overthink it or rewrite it. Let your thoughts flow. The question is: What does my spirit want me to know?

_____

_____

_____

_____

_____

_____

_____

_____

_____

_____

Success

What is your current definition of success?

_____

_____

_____

_____

What might you change your definition of success to?

_____

_____

_____

_____

Clarity – The Missing Piece

Clarity is when life comes into focus

For my clients and me, clarity is the missing piece. We do not know what we want. We have not thought about it. What is in front of us today is our sole focus. Taking the time to envision what our lives could be is just too big for some of us. I heard someone say that we all have a default future or a desired future. Default just happens. Desired is a life based on a vision of what you want your future to look like.

I defaulted for most of my life. My goal in college was to graduate. My friends said, "You are good at this, you should go after this job." I did. A guy said he wanted to marry me. I said "Yes." Then when I started asking myself questions in the middle of the night about, "Is this it for me" – I started to shift to a desired future. My life started to change in momentous ways. I went into life and leadership coaching. I moved to a beach town. I created a community of friends and neighbors that enriched my life. My desired future requires fine-tuning. I am not through. Not finished. I get to make tweaks every year. Writing this book was a desired future decision that wasn't in my original plan. I ask myself what has worked and not worked in the past year? What brought me joy? What would make my life more meaningful? These questions help me fine-tune.

Your desired future will be different than mine. That is ok! You might want to be bolder, less stuck, retire or spend more time with family, work part-time, or change jobs. All of that can happen once you see it and say it out loud. There is research that shows when you get clear about what you want, the Universe or God steps up to help you create it with you. Opportunities just start to happen.

I believe that what you focus on expands. So, if you have clarity, you automatically start to see opportunity and question the status quo.

The saying, "If you don't know where you are headed, any road will get you there" is true. Change does not happen when we are fuzzy. Change happens when we are clear about the end goal.

Creating Your Vision

Ok, the work begins. You need a notebook that is beautiful and a pen that feels good in your hand. You need music and a candle with a scent that soothes you. You need time. This is the hardest part. A Saturday or Sunday afternoon is all you need. Accepting that we deserve to take time just for us is sometimes hard.

1. Now, we brain dump. We need to make room for the creative stuff. You write down whatever is in your head right now—groceries, laundry, dinner, or your list of tasks. Just write it down. Anything we write down gets it out of our head.

2. On to the creative part. Answer the question, "Wouldn't it be cool if?" I read about this in Marie Forleo's book, *Everything is Figureoutable*. "Wouldn't it be cool if I took that trip, bought that house, got that promotion, had some space in my calendar" or whatever comes up. Remember that no one will ever read this. There is nothing too big or too little. There are no rules. Don't overthink this. When you feel that you have exhausted your list, start to highlight, or mark those that excite or inspire you. This is the first step in being free to dream.

3. Next, take a few minutes in that beautiful notebook and answer these questions.
   You do not have to do all of them.
   What matters most? Not what should matter most.
   What would you like to have more of in your life?
   What do you want in your career?
   What would bring more happiness and joy into your life?
   What do you want in your relationships?
   What are your talents? What do others compliment you about?
   What would you most like to accomplish?

4. The fourth creative step is to make a vision board. Now, you need to know that I am not a crafty person. Hobby Lobby™ is not my happy place. Despite my feelings about crafting, I love the end result, so I don't mind going through this process once a year. In late December, my daughter and I get our supplies – poster board, glue sticks and magazines. The process has five parts: flip, rip, sort, arrange and display. The process is to flip through the magazines, rip out pictures or words that inspire you and then start to sort your pictures and arrange them on the poster board. The last part is where the glue stick comes in. Glue down the pictures or sayings that you have chosen.

You have created a vision board. I am proud of you. You don't have to know what the pictures represent for you yet. I make mine which is never as beautiful as the one my artistic daughter creates. I look at my vision board about three or four times a year to remind me of my vision.

On my first vision board years ago, I selected a picture of a woman reading and looking out over water. She seemed peaceful and had room in her life to just be. A year later, my husband and I purchased a beach condominium as a second home. I was sitting on the back porch looking out over the water and it was then that I made the connection. Was that just a coincidence? Maybe or maybe not.

Another version of a vision board can be found on Amazon. It is the Vision Board Kit for Women™. It has pictures and quotes that you choose from to select the ones that speak to you. This kit saves you time and money, everything you need is included, and you can update as often as you like. I am such a nerd that I do both versions.

The last piece is a vision statement. It speaks to what matters most in your life and work. The work you have done on your mind map and vision board will help you write the statement.

A vision statement is written in present tense. It is a statement that is focused on life and professional goals, and it is intended to move you toward your long-term dreams. There is no right statement. It is personal. It only needs to make sense to you. Research has shown that a personal vision statement moves you from stress and anxiety to peace. And a feeling of purpose. It gives you control over your life and starts to move you from a default future to a desired one.

The last part may be the hardest. Share your vision with someone you trust. Allow them to really know you. I know for me, I do not want to share my vision because it might seem silly or unobtainable to someone else. They may make fun of me – "Really, a poster board with pictures is going to change your life?" Visions we can speak out loud are just one more shout-out to God and the Universe to bring it on.

This may seem like a lot. Too much. Just bite off one piece of creating your vision. This process should not feel like work. If the vision board feels like too big a task, you can move right to the statement. Make it work for you.

Intention – How Do You Want to Show Up?

As I have said, we do not get to choose what happens to us, but we do choose how we respond. Intention means to act with purpose. That sounds powerful, doesn't it? It means to start your day with intention. What do you want to be, do, or have? I believe what you put out comes back to you. If you are stressed and anxious at work, you get back stress and anxiety from others. If you choose to show up with an intention to be calm and kind – well, you get the picture. I have been asked what the difference is between purpose and intention. Purpose is why we are doing the stuff and intention is how are we going to do it.

An intention is not a goal. An intention does not have a timeline or end point.

My intention when I used to work in an office was – I show up, speak up and am present. For me all of these are hard. I show up if I have committed to you. I don't always show up when something bad happens. I don't want to say the wrong thing. Speak up even when you don't know what to say or if the question seems silly. Being present is the greatest gift we give another person. It means being there in the moment with them.

I remember someone coming by my office and asking for a moment of my time. I would pretend to be listening, but my mind was on the email I was writing or the meeting I was getting ready to attend. I believe that coaching has become so vital to people because coaches are present for their clients.

My intention when I go to a cocktail party is to be interested and not interesting. I used to hate that cocktail talk. Meaningless and boring, if you ask me. Since my overall theme was to get you to like me, I needed to be charming, funny, and smart. That was exhausting. When I started showing up as myself and I was interested in you is when things started to shift for me. Being curious and open was all it took. Guess what? I had more meaningful conversations and in the end, people liked me better.

My intention when I facilitate a retreat is that I am prepared, open and honest. If my intention is that everyone will love me, I would fail because I don't control that. I can only control how I show up. I want to be able to pivot in a retreat based on the energy of the participants. I always have more exercises planned than we get to. When I held my first women's retreat years ago, I had everything planned down to the minute. I left no room for them to talk! And boy did they. They needed to share their stories. I learned quickly to be flexible and to allow the retreat to unfold. I don't have to teach every lesson. The power of my retreats is not me. It is the connection that women need in their lives and often don't have.

I had a client once that identified what she needed most. It was peace. She had a stressful job and a young child at home. There never seemed to be time for her. Her intention was – "I have peace." She stuck a sticky note to her car dashboard and read it every day. She started to close her door at work when she ate her lunch and to stop reading emails. She asked her husband for a time each week when she could truly unplug. He wholeheartedly agreed because he was craving the same thing. Often, changes that are wanted are just baby steps and asking for what we need. Choosing happy is asking for what we need.

Feelings Come First

In *Fire Starter Sessions* by Danielle Laporte, the concept of core desired feelings was introduced. At least to me. Being someone that has tried to not feel anything, this book said to lean into your feelings. Danielle says, "Knowing how you want to feel is the most potent form of clarity that you can have." Our goals that we want to achieve are intended to get us to feel a certain way. If my goal is to lose fifteen pounds, the feeling I want is confidence. So, how can I feel confident today? What if we reversed the goals and the feelings? What if we decided how we want to feel and then set our goals and strategies? When you are clear about how you want to feel, you can look at every opportunity through the lens of – "How will that make me feel?" There are not wrong feelings or feelings that you should have on your list. We want what we want. You don't have to share this list with anyone unless you decide.

Every year right after finding my word of the year (I'll say more about that later) and my intention, I set out to get clarity about my core desired feelings. I take a list of feelings and circle those that I feel connected to. Then I edit and delete those that are duplicates. What I want are five core desired feelings for the year. The first time I did this exercise, my feelings were flow – abundant – enthusiastic – confident – connected. These all spoke to me. I made a sticky note and put it on my desk. Every morning, I looked at that list and asked myself, "How can I feel those feelings today?" What I realized is that this is choosing happy. I am not waiting for the new promotion at work to feel confident. I can feel confident now. Isn't that amazing?

As I have mentioned, feelings are fuzzy for me. Maybe they are for you too. This exercise makes feelings front and center in your life. Not awards or accomplishments or a raise. Just how you feel.

The thing about these core desired feelings is we must ask ourselves, "What can I do today to feel at least one of them? What baby step can I take that would make me feel the way I want to feel?"

One word that shows up on my list every year is enthusiasm. Enthusiasm is this state of awareness and excitement. For me, it meant realizing that most things are in my control. I can say "No." I can say "Yes" to those things that make me feel enthusiastic. I have started saying "No" to projects that are not a "Hell Yes" for me. Even though the extra money might be nice, I know that I don't want to do them. These projects will drain me of energy and the possibility of saying "Yes" to the next opportunity that is around the corner. It is the fear of scarcity that pushes me to say "Yes." If I believed in abundance and the sense of having enough, then I would not feel so inclined to take on projects that don't light me up. These are the questions I ask:

Does the thought of this project light me up?

Do I want to say no, but feel I should say yes? Why?

Am I willing to say yes to something that is not aligned with my gifts and talents or do I have the guts to say 'this is not mine'?

Perspective is a Choice

I lost my mother when I was twenty-two.

I am lucky to have had my mother for twenty-two years.

Both statements are true. The question is: which perspective do I choose? Part of choosing happy is consciously choosing your perspective.

I did lose my mother when I was twenty-two from pancreatic cancer. When I was nineteen, my mother was having back pain and needed surgery. On the day of the surgery, I was the only family member that was at the hospital. We did not think the diagnosis would be as serious as it turned out to be. After the surgery, the surgeon came out to tell me what he found. His words are written on my brain, "Your mother will die. I cannot tell you when." That was the beginning of the end. This was the first we learned that she had pancreatic cancer.

My sister and I took care of her until her death in January 1982. We were blessed that my mother had great health insurance. We were able to hire nurses to help. It was one of my jobs to get the bills filed with insurance, so that we were able to pay the nurses the next week.

I have never cried over losing my mother. I did not cry at the funeral. I did not cry when we cleaned out her apartment. I didn't cry when my daughter was born (who is named after her) and my mother wasn't there. I regret that I was unable to grieve and let out that pain. I thought that if I opened the flood gates, I would never be able to stop.

I am asked how that experience changed me. I have no idea since I do not know how I would have been if she had lived longer. I don't know how to make gravy. I think she would have taught me that. I didn't always know the rules of life. Could you have a Bloody Mary at night? Or is that just a day drink? I get that it doesn't matter, but at twenty-two it seemed like a big deal. I was writing thank you notes from my first wedding and sympathy notes to the same people. Could you put them in the same note? Who knew, so I did two.

How we perceive a situation directly impacts how we react and the resulting action. Let's say I go with the first perspective about my mother. "I lost my mother when I was only twenty-two." My reaction would be sadness. My actions would be in showing up as a victim and somehow less than.

If I chose the second perspective – "I was lucky to have had my mother for 22 years" — I would feel gratitude. My actions would be more open and generous. The result is that I would feel happy and more available to others.

I am not suggesting that we don't grieve the bad stuff. Acknowledging your feelings and allowing them to come out is vital to healing. Believe me, I know about this one.

Feelings are messy. I have lived in my head and stuffed my feelings so far inside that I cannot even recognize them. The teacher is always the student. I have a lot to learn.

A perspective shift for me was in my relationship with my blended family. There is my father and stepmother, one biological sister, two stepsisters, and their spouses and children. They are all amazing individuals who were kind and generous to me. Every holiday for years, my perspective was that I did not fit in. I guess it was because my mother was gone. They belonged together and I was on the outside looking in. That perspective left me feeling lonely and sad and I believe I showed up seeming aloof and guarded, the result was that I didn't fit in. I created that all by myself. I was hard to get to know.

I decided to change my perspective from "I don't fit in" to "You show up for family." (The new perspective must be believable.) My family did not change but I showed up with no expectations. I shifted, not them. They were always there for me. Open to know me better. Particularly my stepmother. She always wanted a closer relationship with me. I didn't know how to let her in. The change in family holiday events has been huge. A total 360. There are lessons about perspective and vulnerability in this story. My regret is that it took so many years to figure it out. I now have richer, more abundant relationships that enrich my life.

> *"Some people could be given an entire field of roses and only see the thorns in it. Others could be given a single weed and only see the wildflower in it. Perception is a key component to gratitude, and gratitude is a key component to joy."*
> —Amy Weatherly

One Word Changes Everything

I have picked a word of the year for years. I love the process of having a focus or inspiration for the coming year. Choose one word. One word that reminds you about your focus and priority for the coming year. Ask yourself, "What I want to be, do, or have?" Make a list of all the words that come up. Start editing. You want your word to inspire you. To resonate.

Each year I ask myself what matters most—is it Trust? Faith? Abundance, or Peace? These have all been previous words.

My word for 2022 was "BRAVE." For me, that means to be brave in speaking up and in saying "Yes" to things that scare me.

My word for 2023 is "ENOUGH". I am good enough and I have enough.

I pick my word and then find a way to remind me every day. It can be a screen saver or a reminder on my phone. I buy a bracelet every year from myintent.com. I love wearing it.

A word of the year helps you stay focused and moving toward your best life.

Pick a word and see how it helps. I promise you will do life in a more intentional way

Contentment – The Most Powerful Definer of Success

Contentment means that today is good enough. I am satisfied. Today I can see the blessings. It does not mean I have given up or there aren't things I would like to be better at. Many of us believe that contentment is based on our ability to control everything in our lives. Instead, contentment is accepting the current circumstances and being able to say – "today is good."

I know that there are bigger circumstances that get in the way of contentment. I am not the happy fairy that thinks we can happy our way through. I know that bad things happen. And there will certainly be days when contentment is not possible.

I had a client ask me recently, "How do you feel content and not want more?" My answer was easy. **Yes, and Yes!** Yes, today is good and I want more. Yes, I feel satisfied and yet there are bigger things out there for me. Content does not mean sitting on your laurels and giving up on goals and dreams. The opposite is true. Content is the most powerful definer of success.

I spent years in the discontentment phase. If only I was thinner, happier, or more successful. Then I would feel content. Lasting success is based on the feeling of contentment. That is a choice. A choice to see what is working instead of where you have failed.

Exercises

Word of the Year

What is your word of the year?

How will you remind yourself daily?

How will your life be different if you focus on that word?

Intention Setting

Example: Goal – I want to lose fifteen pounds.

Intention – I feel healthy in my body.

Which one feels more inspiring?

Here are some important qualities to remember as you write your intention:

No attachment to an endpoint

No predictable outcome

Present tense

Concise and powerful

How to phrase your intention

Be clear about what you want

Write the statements in the present tense

Use positive language

Express what you feel in as few words as possible

Below are a few exercises that will help you formulate your intentions:

1. What do I want to attract in my life right now?

   (Circle those that resonate)

   O Money and Career

   O Health and Wellness

   O Love and Relationships

   O Spirit and Renewal

   Other - _____

2. What do you want specifically from the list above?

   _____

   _____

   _____

   _____

3. Why is this important to you right now?

   _____

   _____

   _____

   _____

4. If you could achieve these things, how would you feel?

_____

_____

_____

5. What is blocking you now from having this?

_____

_____

_____

_____

Now write your primary intention for your life today.

Use the above exercises to uncover what is true for you. You can have more than one intention or one truth.

_____

_____

_____

_____

Example: _I am free; I am powerful; I am a wise healer who is joyful and compassionate; I am joy and compassion._

Core Desired Feelings

Let's get clear about how we want to feel.

First, write down all the feelings that appeal to you. There is a list of feelings at Practices-FeelingsSensations.pdf (hoffmaninstitute.org) if you need help. Make a list. Start to edit by asking yourself, "Does this feeling mean the same as that one?" This is an intuitive choice. Your gut knows. If it helps, think to yourself that no one will ever read this. Sometimes, this exercise feels selfish. It is not. Give yourself room to honor your feelings.

_____

_____

_____

_____

_____

1. What are five things that will make me feel this way?

_____

_____

_____

_____

2. What are three things I can do this week to create the feelings I want to have?

_____

_____

_____

_____

3. Who do I need more of in my life to have these feelings?

_____

_____

_____

_____

4. Who do I need less of in my life to have these feelings?

_____

_____

_____

_____

Priority – Getting the Right Things Done

Priority—is a thing that is regarded or treated as very important

This section is a game changer. This is where I talk about how to get it all done. We will explore productivity, priority and setting expectations and boundaries for yourself. When we feel that our "busy" makes sense, that it is headed to some end goal, we are choosing happy. When we get the right things done, we are making room for ourselves. A therapist once asked me if I had "room to float." I didn't even know what that meant. Let me say I figured it out. Space and freedom is what we all crave. The goal should not be to get everything done but to find the sense of accomplishment when you get the right things done. Having an empty inbox is not winning.

We all have long lists and want the crazy of our lives to slow down and yet the list keeps getting longer. The first step to creating space in our days is in realizing that all items on your task list are not equal. They don't all require the same amount of attention and time. We must start to look at our lists and ask some questions to determine our priorities.

Questions to Ask Yourself:

Does this need to be done this week?

Is it mine to do?

Can I delegate it?

Can I hire someone to do it?

I was recently asked to be on a panel of women leaders. One of the questions asked was – When have you ever felt that you were doing too much and had to stop and reassess what your priorities were? This made me laugh because I have been doing too much for most of my career. There are several reasons for that, and as I look back, I can see that I created much of my own crazy.

Ten years ago, my business was growing and I couldn't keep up. I was clear that I didn't want employees. There were parts to my one-person business that were draining. They took extra time and kept me from getting the right things done. Someone mentioned a virtual assistant. I started looking around and found mine. We have never met in person, and she has worked for me for the past ten years. I pay for services like creating marketing plans, PowerPoints, website updating and design as well as social media oversight. She allowed me to focus on my priorities. I had no idea that this would change the way I felt at work. I was creating without knowing it – grace and ease at work. More about that later.

When I began coaching, I had a client who had four children under the age of ten and was trying to start a business. Crazy and overwhelmed was normal for her. I suggested she get a housekeeper and part-time help with the kids after school. She immediately told me that it was her job as a mother to get all that done. She believed it would be viewed as failure to say she needed help. After some coaching around her limiting beliefs that were keeping her stuck, she hired both the housekeeper once every other week and a babysitter for a couple of hours during the week. We have stayed in touch, and she says that that decision changed her life in a good way.

The belief that I was an imposter playing the role of a successful businesswoman meant I felt I had to say "Yes" to everything, do it better than anyone else and never let on that I was struggling to get it all done. I had to keep all the plates spinning. Doesn't that sound exhausting? It was. All that activity somehow kept the small voice in my head quiet for a little while, until I dropped a plate or made a mistake, and then the voice was yelling at me again – "See you really are not good enough."

Second, I had priorities but always felt that yours were more important than my own. If you needed my help, I was right there. I felt proud that other people needed me. But, at the end of the day, all your work got done and I was still cringing over my unfinished tasks.

Third, I had never learned to say "No." If I ever said "No," which was seldom, to any request for my time or energy, I added an explanation of all the reasons – real or made up—about why I couldn't do it. "I can't help with that project at this time," would have been enough. But I bet there are times you are asked to take on something in your life or work – that you could say no to – but don't. We don't say no because we're afraid people won't like us, or they will think we don't have it all together, or they will be disappointed. Whatever the reason, we allow others to own our priorities.

Recently, I resigned from a board that I was on. I had made a commitment and felt the need to finish my term. But, I knew that this was draining for me. I knew how I would coach someone else with a similar problem. Finally, after making the decision and telling the other board members I was leaving, I felt such relief. It is nuts how much agony I went through to make that decision. And, the world did not stop. As my sister said, "You are not all that – they will keep going without you." She was right.

Doing what matters most requires us to take inventory of your list and to prioritize it by A, B and C, 1,2,3, or whatever works for you. And then to make sure that you get your A items done every day. B's and C's will always get done. It is the A's that keep us up at night. Now break down your big projects into manageable chunks that are not as overwhelming. For me, the big project might be – "create a presentation." That is big and there are lots of steps. If that was one of my tasks, I would procrastinate. I know myself. To get it done, I break that down into bite-size items like – write an agenda, do the PowerPoint, create handouts, and get the supplies needed. None of those feel overwhelming.

Grace and Ease is the Path

We have been taught that life is hard. Getting ahead is hard. Let me be clear, life can be hard. Work can be demanding. It is up to us to decide what our part is in our demanding jobs. Are we saying "Yes" too often? Are we spending too much time on each task, even those that should be quick and easy? What is standing in the way of working with grace and ease? I am told all the time by my clients that their job is demanding, the tasks and projects are overwhelming, and that they have no control over changing that. I know it feels that way, but I believe there are some pieces to your own crazy that you can control. Only you can figure out what change is possible for you.

For instance, interruptions are a big distractor from productivity. We have been taught that closing our door or being inaccessible is a bad thing. The truth is that after every interruption it can take up to fifteen minutes to get back to where you were before the interruption. Yes, some interruptions are necessary. But, some can be postponed to a later time. "Can I get with you later today?" is a reasonable response to the question, "Can I have a minute of your time?"

Grace and ease are the path to a calm and contented life. I know this is true and I know it is available to all of us. We have to look for what areas of work and life can be handled differently.

I remember when I bought into a company in my thirties. I was one of two owners of an association management company. Everyone said that I would have to work long hours to make the company successful. To be honest, owning my own business was easier than working for someone else. Sure, there was pressure and different demands, but those demands were mine.

My business partner said when we started that we would have balanced lives. We would close at a normal time. I learned a lot from watching her manage her life. She taught me to choose happy, find fun and do great work. One of the perks of having your own business is to create it the way you want it to be. She gave me permission to trust myself and to know that working late did not equate with success. Setting our priorities and getting the right things done would be the barometer of our success.

Grace means to act with kindness and compassion to others and, more importantly, to yourself. We are always our own worst critic. Give yourself grace when you don't get it right. Give yourself grace when you don't do what you said you were going to do.

Ease is a quiet confidence, working through your daily demands knowing that the big stuff will get done. We can get addicted to that crazy out-of-control feeling. We can get addicted to being busy. There is an adrenaline rush when we have a deadline and are pushing to meet it. Feeling out of control and overwhelmed happens to all of us. If it happens to you most of the time, you need to examine that. What is the payoff for putting things off 'til the end? Dr. Phil says "We don't do things that don't work for us." Now you can ask yourself, does this still work for me? Maybe it is time to examine how you are contributing to your own sense of crazy.

In living with grace and ease, you must make room for you. As I stated earlier, you have to say "No" to make room for "Yes." When someone tells me no because they are not taking anything else on, I respect them. I am not mad. They have healthy boundaries.

Boundaries are a form of self-care. Setting boundaries protects your time and energy. When we say "Yes" to something we are always saying "No" to something else.

Healthy emotional **boundaries** mean you value your own feelings and needs and you're not responsible for how others feel or behave. For me, one of the hardest things that I have had to learn is that I am not responsible for others' happiness. One of my coaches said the most profound thing to me. When someone you know is upset, ask yourself this question –"Is this mine? Is this mine to fix?" Most of the time, it is not. I can listen and support, but not make it all better. Letting go of my need to keep everyone else happy has been a game-changer. Thanks, Michelle Vos.

Setting healthy boundaries is one way for you to choose happy. Here are some examples. Are there two or three that you are willing to adopt?

I won't check email after 6 pm.

I won't work on weekends unless there is a deadline that demands it.

I will make time for my health practices.

I will be present for my children and partner.

I will put me on my calendar.

I will speak up and ask for what I want and need.

I will become comfortable saying "No".

The Big Rocks Experiment

The most powerful way to get the right things done is by putting your personal priorities on your calendar first. Dinner with your husband, exercise, friendships, spiritual practices—they give your life meaning. They matter and they won't happen if not scheduled.

I have a yoga class that I enjoy on Monday mornings. There is no reason that I can't block out that time. But, if one of my clients asks to have a call, I am likely to cancel that yoga class. I am not good at keeping my commitments to myself. Are you? I am committed to making that yoga class this year.

Stephen Covey talked about your big rocks in the *Seven Habits of Highly Effective People.* He used a big jar to make his case. He said that we must put in the big rocks first (family, friends, spiritual practices, health, rest, and fun). When you put those in first, the medium rocks (meetings, projects, obligations, interruptions) will fit in the jar. Then the little rocks (emails, phone calls and social media pings) will fill in around the big rocks. If the big rocks don't go in first, they won't fit later. I encourage you to watch videos that demonstrate how this works. Please scan this QR code to view one video that I like on YouTube:

Spending a few minutes over the weekend and adding your big rocks to your calendar is vital to choosing happy. If you don't schedule your big rocks, they won't get done. Think about your life if you got all the work stuff done all the time, but didn't spend time with family and friends, didn't read that book, exercise or just take time to float.

Alignment is Living Your Purpose

One question I always ask my clients is, "Are your job responsibilities and your gifts and talents in alignment? Does the work you do use your gifts?" One barometer you can use to test your alignment is an exercise by Michael Bungay Stanier in his book *Do Great Work*.

You start with a blank piece of paper. You make a big circle. You divide your circle into three sections. These sections are probably not going to be the same size. The sections represent (1) your great work, when the task is effortless and you can lose yourself in it, (2) good work, work that you can do well but it doesn't light you up and (3) bad work, including those tasks you procrastinate on. You hate doing them. These are also tasks in which you are not proficient. Make a list of all your tasks that encompass your job and add them in the right section of the circle. The point of the exercise is to look at this list and note how many tasks are in each category. First, look at the work you hate doing. How can you move any of that off your list? We may have the belief that we have to do everything and it doesn't matter where it fits in the circle. I say that we might have some options if we could open our minds to possibility.

Do you have about 25% of tasks under great work? If so, you are doing well. If not, you might want to examine your position. Maybe there is a way to realign your position to include more of what you consider your great and good work.

I was not in alignment for years. I was doing very detailed meeting and association management. It took everything I had to get the work done. But I did not even realize it until I changed jobs and was more of a strategist and planner. I now accept that details are not my thing. I don't beat myself up about it, I just have others go behind me and check for those kinds of mistakes.

Big Three

Michael Hyatt, founder and CEO of Michael Hyatt & Company, is a popular speaker and has published many books about time management and leadership. In his book, *Free to Focus*, he talks about reviewing your work at the beginning of the week and developing your Big Three list. Which big projects need to be done this week? If we can see our priorities, it allows us to focus on them without distraction. One of my beliefs is what we focus on will get done. I start my week with a big three list and then each day, I do my big three list for that day. It keeps me connected to those things that will move my business and life forward.

Our Buckets

How heavy are all the buckets that you have to carry in your life? Buckets are the roles and responsibilities we all have. Mine would be:

Work

Wife

Mother

Daughter

Friend

Health

Boards/Community Commitments

We tend to think that our buckets are ours to carry. I believe we get to decide which buckets we will carry and which ones should be let go. Ask yourself: is it yours to carry? Are some buckets heavier than others?

But, for the heavy buckets that you can release, ask yourself these questions. Who will be affected if I let it go? How am I being affected by continuing to carry it? What are the consequences of just saying "No"?

Clutter—What to Do with All the Stuff?

All the mental and physical stuff that invades and fills up our drawers, closets, inboxes, desks and all the stuff in our heads. Clutter is spiritually heavy. It is the result of a postponed decision. "I don't know what to do with that so I will keep it, file it, or store it."

As fans of the TV show from Marie Kondo and the author of the bestseller, *The Magic of Tidying Up*—many of us have been on this bandwagon for a while. "Does it spark joy?" That is the question that we have been told to ask our stuff to decide if we should keep it or not.

My husband and I downsized a few years ago. We moved to a townhouse that is about half the size of our other home. While this is a decision we made with enthusiasm – the issue of stuff was the hardest to tackle. I pride myself on my ability to edit – get rid of things that no longer serve me. And yet, letting go of excess dishes, clothes, and knick-knacks was harder than I imagined. My husband is very attached to his stuff. Letting go hurts him – he agonizes over these decisions. I have watched him hold one thing in his hand for fifteen minutes, pondering the uses of it, or what he might do with it if he saves it, or who might use it if he lets it go.

I know that for many people this is hard. If you are someone that has a hard time dealing with letting go – I get it. I also understand that there is a lightness that comes from being able to open that kitchen drawer that holds all the stuff (menus, extra pens, chargers, lighters, etc.) that won't go anywhere else. Or to be able to move your hangers around in your closet with ease. There is lightness and freedom after you make those choices to give your life space. It is worth the work!

There are two kinds of clutter—physical and mental. I don't want to ignore the significance of mental clutter. That tape we have running in our heads of things we need to do, things we can't forget, or just more stuff. It takes up space and keeps us in a state of anxiety and stress.

Now is a good time to tackle some of the clutter in your life. Think about where to start. Pick something manageable in a few hours. Is it that kitchen drawer, a closet, or your desk at work? Set aside the time. Get your supplies ready – garbage bags, boxes, containers, etc. Don't overthink it. You probably don't need it if you haven't used it, worn it, or looked for it in over a year. If you haven't used that crock pot in ages– let it go. After you finish, celebrate that space that you have opened in your life. Pledge not to fill it back up with new stuff.

I send a lot to Goodwill. It makes me feel that I am

not throwing away something but moving it along for someone else to use.

Clearing clutter frees your spaces – your house, your office and your mind leaving you room to breathe, relax and enjoy. Make a promise to yourself to start this month. It will make a difference in how you feel in life and work. It is another way to choose happy.

I will continue to ask myself, "Does this bring me joy?"

Batching Creates Space in Your Calendar

You have probably heard of the concept of batching like activities together. For instance, if I have to go to the bank, UPS, and the grocery store – it makes sense to do all of these errands in one trip. Not three. I try to batch coaching calls on Tuesday, Wednesday, and Thursday. I like to keep Monday and Friday open for paperwork and organization. I also batch any videos or writing that require me to be creative or cute.

What if you had one day a week when you do not schedule meetings? That day would be for the deep dive stuff – planning, project work and organization. Think about dressing down on the no-meetings day. I think there is freedom in knowing that your week is scheduled to serve you.

The best way to start to batch your work is to list your typical responsibilities and identify where it makes sense to combine them. I created an ideal work week for myself. This helped me start to be intentional about my calendar. You can see mine following.

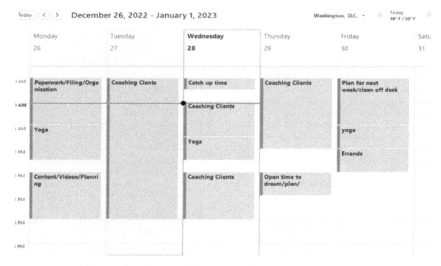

Goals – What Do You Want to Accomplish?

I strongly believe that the exercises in this book have prepared you to create meaningful goals. Vision is the why. Goals are the how. Goals are more deliberate than desires or intentions. Goals should be specific and clear. You don't need twenty-five goals. Your goals should motivate you and inspire you. Imagine with each goal, what would that feel like when you achieve it? I suggest creating quarterly goals. That works for me. At the end of this chapter is the form that I use to set mine. I hope it is helpful to you.

By looking back over the exercises that you have done so far, you will have a sense of what your goals might be.

Mind Mapping

Vision Board

Vision Statement

Word of the Year

Intention Setting

Core Desired Feelings

My "Doing What Matters" Tools

SaneBox (sanebox.com) is a tool to automate email and put order into your inbox. It identifies important messages, hides distractions, has a Do Not Disturb section, banishes annoying senders, reminds you to follow up, and more. I have paid for this tool for three years and my inbox is down by 60%. I have a SaneLater folder where emails are sent that might be of value like newsletters and SaneNews which is where most of my emails get sent. It identifies marketing emails, possible junk and sends them to this folder bypassing my inbox. This has been a lifesaver for me. As my friend says, it keeps me from going down the rabbit trail.

Outlook Tasks. I am a productivity junkie. I believe that any new organizational system is going to be the one. It will keep me focused, organized, and make my life better. For me, Outlook Tasks is the cornerstone of my organization.

Any planning system will work if you are consistent. I have tried every day-planner out there. They all worked for a while. I have so many productivity books I can't count. In the end, I have gone back to Outlook tasks. It is the most underutilized tool of Outlook, and it works for me for many reasons. I have so much to say about the tasks tool that I've added a section below.

If you have not used Tasks before, I recommend you play around with it. I like to see my tasks right beside my emails. To do that, go to View and click on the To-Do bar. Voila – it will appear.

Tasks can be added as you think of them. I like to put a date by each task. And, then I can see what I must do today. This keeps me focused. I can also prioritize each task as low, normal, or high. If I have a task for Monday and I don't get it done, it immediately shows up on Tuesday. That way, I don't forget about it. I never have to rewrite my list. I also have some tasks with no date because they are just ideas about things I would like to do in the future, but don't know when.

Jules Acree Notion Templates. Jules Acree (julesacree. com) is a lifestyle expert who has helped me get my personal life in order. I love her Notions Templates that help organize goals, lists, movies, books, recipes and so much more. She says, "I help you create more time, space, and energy through intentional systems and rituals that simplify your life."

Remarkable. How often have you written something down and then a few weeks later, you can't find it anywhere? Last year, I purchased a Remarkable for myself. It has changed my notetaking. Remarkable is a digital notebook that keeps me organized. It has saved me hours of searching for information. Everything is in this digital notebook. I open a page and start writing. That same page can be emailed to me or changed to text. Here is what it does:

- Takes your handwritten notes and converts them to text.

- Organizes your notes into folders and is accessible on all devices.

I use this tool in my note-taking for clients, potential clients, my big three lists, and ongoing projects. It has replaced those spiral notebooks for me.

Outlook Management

What I know about Outlook and time management I learned from the best, Kimberly Medlock. She is a speaker and author. Her book, *Smarter Work Habits that Matter*, is filled with actionable and smart productivity tools. She is an expert on making Outlook work for you. I had the privilege of working with her for several years as a trainer.

Outlook from Microsoft is an email program, but it does so much more than most of us take advantage of. Let me share a few of my tips that keep me on track.

There are only two ways to get more time - eliminate and simplify. This applies to email. We are all inundated with an abundance of emails. Our inboxes are overflowing. My guess is that most of those emails are not a priority. Email is a communication tool. It is not what we do. However, most people check their email every 5 minutes. Obviously, we know instinctively that this can't be the best way to manage our day. And yet, the fear of missing something important keeps us tied to it.

Here are some tips to make Outlook work for you.

Clean Out Your Inbox

Delete – Just do it. The first sweep through emails

is to see what can be deleted. One secret is to sort your inbox by the "from" field. This allows you to see where there are several emails from the same person or company that could be moved to a folder or deleted.

Unsubscribe – make sure those emails don't come back.

Rules – the most important tool you can learn about is setting up rules to make your inbox more manageable. A rule can be set up to send all emails where you are cc'ed to go to a folder called the cc folder. A rule can be set up to send all Chicos and J.Jill emails to go to a folder called Shopping. A rule can be set up to send all social media emails to a folder called Social. All these tips can reduce your inbox.

Many people are scared to move an email out of their inbox because they might forget where they put it. Keeping all emails in your inbox actually creates more work for you. Research says that we will re-read an email two to three times that stays in our inbox. Move it to a folder instead.

Managing Your Inbox

Keep your emails as simple as possible.

If you want fewer emails, send fewer. Have you gotten an email and then replied with thanks? Quit doing that. You are just adding to their inbox madness.

Don't "reply all". Only reply to a group email to the people that need to know. I have seen an email chain about what everyone wants to order for the lunch meeting. I don't care if you want the turkey or ham sandwich. Only the organizer needs to know.

When an email chain has gone back and forth twice and is still not resolved, pick up the phone.

How to Make Folders Work Effectively

I learned this from Kimberly Medlock. She said to think of your folders as drawers in a file cabinet. That means grouping your folders into a more manageable order. I have a folder for clients, projects, pending, reading, coaching, and personal. There are subfolders under each of those.

I have three folders that I created to make my inbox more manageable. They are pending, reading and follow-up. If I read an email that can be delayed, this is where I park it.

- Pending is for those emails that I need to keep close, like items ordered, doctor appointment notices, or travel emails.

- A reading folder is for all those newsletters and emails that I want to learn more about.

- And, my follow-up folder is for those emails that I need to follow up on but not today.

The last tip for folders is that, as you know, folders show up in alphabetical order. What if your most used folder starts with a "T"? You would have to scroll down to find it constantly. That takes time. If you put a numeric number or a symbol in front of your folder name, you have now moved it to the top of the list.

Now for the best part. On your navigation bar, click

on your email address above your inbox. This is your Outlook Today. It takes out all the clutter and shows you what is on your plate for today. You can customize this page. I love to start my day with this page open to see my schedule and tasks.

Sunday, December 18, 2022 Customize Outlook Today ...

Calendar	Tasks	Messages	
Today	☐ Put all clients in CA/Taylor, Timothy, Eric and add new LC staff (12/18/2022)	Inbox	5
Multi-day event Dan in Virginia	☐ Edit priority (12/18/2022)	Drafts	0
Multi-day event Storey - here		Outbox	0
Monday			
All day event Finish truth			
Tuesday			
All day event Anne Fitzgerald's birthday			
▶ 12:00 PM - 1:15 PM Gentle Yoga: Flow			
1:30 PM - 2:30 PM Coastal Pharmacy			

Keystone Habits

Charles Duhigg, author of *The Power of Habit*, talks about the idea of keystone habits. Have you ever wondered why your New Year's resolutions never seem to stick? We all know the steps to living a healthier life, how to be more organized, and how to care for ourselves. I know all of them and yet I don't do them. I have long-held habits that keep me stuck. Changing a habit is so hard to do. I know that eating in front of the television is a bad habit. Even though health is a priority of mine, I sit in front of the TV while I eat. I can say that I am going to get up early to exercise. My habit is to sleep until I wake up and then sit with my coffee. Changing that seems impossible. Our brains are programmed to do things the way we have always done them. The brain is looking to make fewer choices and do more things automatically.

According to Charles Duhigg, new habits spark a *chain reaction that help other good habits take hold*. In other words, building a keystone habit is like knocking down the biggest domino — it will automatically knock down the other dominoes as well.

Some keystone habits that are worth exploring are exercise, prayer or meditation, morning rituals, and sleep. Which keystone habit do you want to start with? Don't take on more than two at a time. Just do those new habits for three months and then add a new one. It has been proven that it takes sixty-seven days for a new habit to take hold.

Dare's Top Ten Productivity Tips

1. A planning tool is a must. A yellow pad of paper is not a system.

2. Start your day with an intention and quiet time

3. Use your first two hours wisely. Most of us are the most productive in the morning.

4. Schedule times to check email and turn off notifications.

5. Plan for a no-meetings day each week on your calendar and block it out.

6. Clear the clutter a little at a time.

7. Don't overthink your emails. Reread once and hit send.

8. If an email is long and detailed, be sure to put the most relevant information on the first page.

9. If the email will take two minutes or less to complete – just do it. If it will take longer, put it on your task list.

10. Put a two-hour block on your calendar for deep dive time. That is where solutions to problems happen; where creativity is allowed to flow, and where strategy and vision are created.

Exercises

What are your "big rocks"? Those things that sustain your life and make it meaningful? I break mine down in three key areas: Physical, Mental and Spiritual. Feel free to make up your own big rock list.

Big Rock 1

_____

_____

_____

_____

Big Rock 2

_____

_____

_____

_____

Big Rock 3

_____

_____

_____

_____

Gifts and Talents

What are your strengths?

(Another way to answer this is "what do people tell you you're good at - even if you don't agree?")

_____

_____

_____

What are your interests?

What do you do in your free time?

_____

_____

_____

What is your purpose?

Oprah Winfrey said. "Align your personality with your purpose, and no one can touch you." Living my best life is my purpose. When I am in the zone of living my best life, I am a better mother, wife, friend and coach. Purpose does not have to be big and scary. It is just the contribution you want to make in your world. Write down your purpose in the space below.

_____

_____

_____

Quarterly Priorities

Staying on Track

Quarter: _____

Goal: _____

Date Completed by: _____

Action Steps

1. _____

2. _____

3. _____

4. _____

5. _____

Goal: _____

Date Completed by: _____

Action Steps

1. _____

2. _____

3. _____

4. _____

5. _____

Goal: _____

Date Completed by: _____

Action Steps

1. _____

2. _____

3. _____

4. _____

5. _____

Goal: _____

Date Completed by: _____

Action Steps

1. _____

2. _____

3. _____

4. _____

5. _____

Habit Changes

What is the keystone habit you are ready to tackle?

_____

How will you measure success in creating this new habit?

_____

How will you hold yourself accountable? How will you keep this habit alive?

Note to Self

When things feel overwhelming, remember -

One thought at a time.

One task at a time.

One day at a time.

Truth – Speak Your Truth Even When Your Voice Trembles

"Each time a woman stands up for herself,
without knowing it possibly, without claiming
it, she stands up for all women."
— *Maya Angelou*

What if you were your own best advocate, asking for what you need and having more support from the people in your world? Speaking up is crucial to having more peace of mind, success and most importantly - happiness. The secret is that you always had the key to your best life. It is in asking for what you want out loud. In this section, I give you tools and strategies to speak up in your life.

Years ago, a friend of mine gave me this quote – "Speak your truth even when your voice trembles" — on a cocktail napkin when I was going through a very difficult time. I kept it for years. I loved the simplicity and the magnitude of it. Many of us talk ourselves out of speaking up. *It is not the right time; it doesn't matter anyway; even if I say something nothing will change.* So, we let it go. We keep it to ourselves. A fellow coach compared unsaid feelings to trying to hold down a beachball underwater. You know how hard it is to do. We hold on tightly with both hands and we apply pressure to keep it down. Eventually, it escapes and jumps out of the water. It makes a big splash. We do that with our feelings that are stuffed and not talked about. One day we explode. Usually to the ones we trust and love the most.

I coach clients around the concept of speaking up in their life and work. Speaking your truth will move your life forward more quickly than any other strategy in this book. We must believe the following:

We matter.

What we feel matters.

What we need matters.

What we want matters.

What hurts us matters.

A few years ago, I was in one place and my husband was in another. I missed him and really wanted him to come visit over that weekend. I didn't want to put pressure on him by asking, so instead I simply said, "Are you coming this weekend?" and he said, "Probably not." I wanted to ask him. And, yet I was afraid to ask. How silly. I love the sentiment that I hear from clients, "If he loved me, he would just know." I am sure I said that when I was younger. How? How would he know? Unless we express ourselves. In the end, I pushed myself and told him that it would mean a lot to me if he would come and that I missed him. He came. He didn't know that it mattered. I spoke my truth. Speaking your truth is powerful and liberating. The other side effect was that my husband felt needed. That was what he needed too.

Speaking up is hard for most women I know. *Be nice.* That is what we were taught. Be nice meant to be quiet and go along. At least, that is how I interpreted it. For most of my life, not speaking up has been the cause of much of my discomfort and unhappiness. Remember, I have been married three times. I was nice in each marriage. I crave harmony and that has kept me from having difficult conversations. I thought success in relationships meant not ever fighting or even disagreeing. How wrong is that? Not being myself has given me temporary harmony but at what cost? The best conversations are those that we are afraid to have. When we don't know what to say.

I have talked about vulnerability. It is relevant here because, in difficult conversations, we must show up and be vulnerable. Here are some examples:

I was hurt by what you said.

I am afraid that we are not ok.

I need you.

I love you.

I am not happy.

All hard conversations to have. One underlying limiting belief is that you are about to hurt the other person. The belief is that it is easier to pay the price for your happiness rather than take the chance that someone else might be hurt. That is an assumption on your part. My guess is that the person you need to talk to already knows something is up and is left to figure it out on their own. That can be more hurtful in the end.

This is what I used to do. I had the difficult conversation in my head and told myself what I believed you would say back. By the time I had completed this make-believe conversation, I concluded that the conversation wouldn't go well, so I swept it under the rug. Damn, do I have some lumpy carpet! My family didn't speak up either. When they finally did, there was yelling involved.

I knew what I didn't want. And yet, I was depriving myself of deeper connections with family and friends. I created a sense of loneliness that has pervaded my life. This feeling of not fitting in.

Pendulum – Two Sides to the Same Coin

Let me be clear. I am not suggesting that there are not times when doing what others want is not the right thing to do. Being generous and kind and loving is who we are. I don't want to ever lose that and don't want that for you. Going on vacation to a place that might not be your choice but will bring your children joy and memories is absolutely the right choice. Giving of your time when you don't have the time might very well be the next right thing to do. Giving of our time and attention to our friends, family, and neighbors is a good thing – most of the time. So, what am I saying? Are you confused? It is this: on one end of the pendulum is the doormat who never speaks up for themselves and always does what others want of them. The other end is the person who never gives in, never says "yes" to anything that is not on their list of wants and desires. Find the blend – the balance. Give in some, speak up some. Pick your battles. Give in on the things that are not crucial to your happiness and stand up for those things that are. This is the hard part. We have tended to live at one end or the other. Which way do you need to shift?

Difficult Conversations

In the book, *Crucial Conversations* by Kerry Patterson, Joseph Grenny, Ron McMillan and Al Switzer, they discuss the importance of starting with heart when preparing for a crucial conversation. You do that by asking yourself, "How can I say what I need to say with kindness?" The secret is in saying it when it needs to be said and not when you explode because you didn't say it sooner. Speaking up in a crucial conversation is a thoughtful, planned conversation.

Examples of crucial conversations:

Ending a relationship.

Asking a friend to repay a loan.

Talking with a co-worker who behaves offensively.

Resolving custody or visitation issues with an ex-spouse.

Before beginning the crucial conversation, ask yourself three questions.

What is my intention?

What do I really want for myself?

What do I need from the other person?

The Framework for Difficult Conversations

In her book, *Fierce Conversations* by Susan Scott, she talks about how to have difficult conversations. What are the steps?

Name the issue – Name the behavior that is causing the problem.

Select a specific example - be specific and succinct.

Describe your emotions about the issue – Emotions are powerful and can't be disputed because they are yours. They may not have been the intention of the other person, but the emotion is how you felt.

Identify your contribution to this problem – what did you do that contributed to the issue? Accept your part and apologize for it.

Indicate your wish to resolve the issue – Is this what I want to resolve?

Invite the other person to respond – I would like to know your perspective. What is going on with you?

Resolution – How are we both going to do this differently moving forward?

My recommendation is always to start small in speaking up. Start with the easy stuff. Speak up that you don't want Mexican food again this week. When we look for non-significant opportunities to speak up, it is like using a muscle that hasn't been used recently. After time, it will become stronger. And you will speak up more and often. It is okay to say to someone, "I am working on speaking my truth and it might not come out right. Bear with me." We deserve to express what matters most to us. What we want most is to be seen and heard. The only one in the way of that happening is you. Believe me, I know this is true.

Speaking Up for Your Friends

Friends are the secret sauce of life. My girlfriends are worth speaking up for and I bet yours are too. Making time for my friends is a priority for me. I don't see it as taking away time from my family. I see it as filling my tank, so I have more to give.

I have been blessed with girlfriends. Maybe it is because of losing my mother that I am so aware of the value they add to my life. I always say "I am filled up" when I come home from a visit or weekend with my girlfriends.

For my 50th birthday, I invited my girlfriends to go to the beach for a long weekend. I worried that they would feel burdened and only come because they didn't want to let me down. I almost didn't ask. I did ask and they all came. That began a tradition that has lasted many years. I know that it means as much to them as it does to me. They call me the glue. I book the condo and collect the money. The truth is that I do it for my own happiness. It is just a few days where we laugh, forget to wear make-up, watch movies, and share our lives with each other. I created that. What could you create that would add happiness to your life?

I have women leaders as clients who know that friendships are important. They just can't find time. Between work and home there just is no room for another commitment. There is also guilt. Do you have that? Shouldn't I be with my children? Or—I should be doing …? You fill in the blank. My belief is that when you spend time with friends you are filling your cup and you will be overflowing when you get home. You will be a better mother, wife, leader, etc. The result of doing things for you is a happier you. Choosing happy is a good choice every time.

I keep a connection list. These are friends that I want to

stay in touch with. I get busy just like you and don't check on my friends as often as I would like. I keep that list to remind me that I want to stay connected to these women. I believe what you put out comes back to you. If I stay in touch with them, they will stay in touch with me.

Speaking Up for Your Health

When we are sick or not at our best, every area of our life suffers. Taking the time to be our healthiest needs to be our priority. What have you been putting off for your own health that needs to be addressed? So many times, we are on the back burner of our own lives. Making time for ourselves feels overwhelming. We let our commitments go that we make to ourselves in order to meet the expectations of everyone else. It bears repeating – we can't give from an empty cup. What have you been avoiding or putting off?

Doctor Appointments

Time for exercise

Meal prepping

Looking into that gym membership

Creating a quiet space in your bedroom for optimal sleep and rest

Taking that walk

Thought about yoga but haven't tried it

It is time to put our health needs on the list and speak up about them to your family. They matter. I am certainly teaching what I need to learn. I will break commitments to myself but keep commitments made to others. I need to practice what I preach.

The other thing about health—and that includes weight—is to remember that this is a marathon, not a sprint. I am overweight and have been since birth. I weighed eleven pounds. I know. My father said that when he went to the window to see me, the nurse came out and asked if he was related to the baby. He explained that he was the father. The nurse said she was tired of carrying me around since everyone wanted to see the infant that weighed this much. I was doomed from the start.

I know I am not alone when I tell you that I have gone on every diet imaginable. They all work for a few weeks and then I would hit the plateau. The negative self-talk starts. The "I don't have the willpower it takes to lose weight" thoughts. "I never stick to anything." I am looking for the sprint win. For me, there is a belief that someone out there, some diet guru, has the answer for my body. That they are the experts and if I would only listen and follow their rules, my problems would be gone. I wonder why I have bought into that. I am the expert on this body. I know when I eat too much. I know when I am stress eating. I know when I feel light and energetic. My promise to myself is to take control of my health. The scale is not my friend. I have a love/hate relationship with it. Why does it define me? Maybe this will resonate with you.

I am working to make peace with this body and to be kinder to myself. We will see if that helps. The continuous beating myself up is not working. I am in this for the marathon. Let's keep talking!

Do the "Next Right Thing"

Do the next right thing has been a catchphrase for my friends and clients for years. It means simply that when we feel stuck with the long list or the big decisions that are looming, just take one action. Action leads to the next action. When you take one action – any action will move you forward. This motto has served me well in my life. During difficult times, I can remember thinking about that one small step. Sometimes, that is the only thing that needs doing today.

My Defining Moments

When I had accepted the position of Director of Tourism for Mississippi, having been appointed by the Governor, I was 39 and this felt big. The way people treated me changed immediately. I was given suites in hotels, status seating in restaurants, and more. No one mispronounced my name, which had been common before. I quickly believed the hype that I was all that.

One night I was visiting the city where my parents lived. I invited my father and stepmother to dinner. When we got to the restaurant in the beautiful city of Bay St. Louis, Mississippi we immediately were sent over a bottle of wine and an appetizer. I was thinking that my dad was so proud. That is not quite what he was thinking. He pointed at the appetizer and wine and said, "All of this is about what is behind your name. It is not about you. When the title goes away, so does all the stuff." He went on to say that I should enjoy every moment. At that moment a little pin burst my ego bubble. And boy was he right. I left that position with friendships that lasted longer than the job. That was winning and lasting. The others were just fringe benefits.

Operation: Time Off

Once, a friend suggested that I take a month off. Who can do that? My beliefs were that it was unattainable for me no matter how glorious it sounded. Freedom and space have always been values of mine. My sister is a teacher and I have always envied her three-month summer break.

I decided to consider it. I started to float the idea by my clients. Not one client seemed uncomfortable with the idea. They turned out to be my most encouraging cheerleaders.

This is one of my defining moments because I asked for what I wanted. It felt extravagant. And yet, I asked.

The ego voice in my head was saying - "You can't take a month off. Your clients will leave you and find another coach."

My spirit voice was saying - "You are not all that. Your clients will be fine if they don't talk to you for a month. They will see that you are practicing what you preach."

Luckily, the spirit voice won. I am so glad I listened and didn't pay attention to the ego voice.

It was exactly what I needed to recharge and reset. What do you need to recharge? Not everyone can take a month off, but how much time can you take off? Look at your calendar and get back with me.

Some options for your own Operation: Time Off:

Weekend all alone surrounded by books, journals, music, movies, and time to daydream.

Girls Trip

Romantic Getaway

One day a month off – doing nothing that you should

do – only do things that are fun and fill you up.

An afternoon at the movies all alone – you, the big screen, and popcorn.

Five Elementary Schools in Six Years

Our family moved a lot when I was younger. My father worked for Sears and he was transferred a lot. To move up, meant moving. I was shy and changing schools was a major area of stress and anxiety for me. I went to five elementary schools. I had to be the new kid five times. This meant developing my own armor to get through that walk through the cafeteria trying to look nonchalant as I had nowhere to sit. Something shifted in me. Some fundamental thought that I had to take care of myself. That the friends I made at the last school were gone and now I would have to start over. This was certainly way before Facebook. My coping mechanism became food. Something that was always available and soothing to me.

When we moved, we just left everyone behind. It seemed to my eight-year-old mind, that people came and went. The last move was when I was in sixth grade. I remember the first day clearly. I had on a green jumper and pigtails. My teacher was Mr. Anderson. He did his best to make me feel comfortable. I just didn't want to stand out. Blending in was the goal. It was particularly difficult. That was my last new school experience – thank goodness. To this day, being the new person at a party, church or group is still a sixth-grade throwback for me.

What Makes Me Happy?

We all need to know what is on our list. I didn't know what choosing happy looked like for me for many years.

Today, the list is easy:

A hot bath with scented bubbles

A candle burning in my kitchen and fresh flowers on my counter

Music playing in my home

Order – making sure all my stuff is in its place

Reading a good book

Chatting with a friend

Long talks with my daughter

Date night with Husband #3

Keep this list in your notes on your phone and when you find yourself bored, alone or sad – pull up your list and pick something that brings you happiness.

My Truth

My life is happy and messy.

I use humor to deflect getting too close.

I have always had people that believed in me more than I believed in myself.

I have experienced pain, loss, and sadness.

I survived cancer.

My glass is ½ full.

I am impulsive and do too much online shopping.

I love my family and friends more than they know.

Journaling is Another Way to Speak Up

In *Perfect Pitch: How to Speak Up for Yourself in Everyday Relationships* by Marsha Lichtenstein PhD, she writes about the value and importance of journaling. I have journaled since I was in my twenties. I know that all those entries were for me and me alone. They have clarified so many moments in my life. Marsha says, "Use a Journal to Record Your Progress. A journal is a great transformational tool because it's a mirror. In a journal, we can identify both our current state and where we want to go."

I think journaling gets a bad rap. I hear, "I don't have time. I don't know what to write." Journaling is not a chore. It is not another responsibility. It is a tool when you feel the need to see a situation outside of yourself. Writing it down is therapeutic and healing. It is a way to let go of pain. It is a way to celebrate those small or big wins. It is a record of your life, feelings, accomplishments and even disappointments.

We have discussed the big and small ways you can start to speak up for yourself. We are all at different points on the pendulum. It is interesting to me that many strong, successful women can speak up at work but not at home. Why is that?

Speaking up can be hard at first. I urge you to start. Look for opportunities to ask questions or offer advice or ask for what you want or need. Start small. If we believed we mattered, we would not have such a hard time. Think about that.

Exercises for Truth

Who is on your connection list?
Who do you want to remember to stay in touch with this year?

_____

_____

_____

_____

_____

_____

Rate yourself on the pendulum of speaking up from 1-5. One means you rarely speak up and five means you always speak up.

_____

Where do you want to move to?

_____

Who do you need to have a difficult conversation with?

_____

_____

What do you need to say?

_____

_____

What is on your "choosing happy" list?

_____

_____

_____

_____

_____

_____

_____

_____

_____

_____

_____

Friends

What could you do this year to make time for your friends?

_____

_____

_____

_____

_____

_____

What are your defining moments?

_____

_____

_____

_____

_____

_____

What is your Operation: Time Off Plan?

_____

_____

_____

_____

_____

_____

Health Plans – List three things you commit to do to be healthier.

_____

_____

_____

"You can't keep getting mad at people for sucking the life out of you if you keep giving them the straw."
—*@thewirdz*

Living and Leading by Design

This book is filled with exercises whose goal is to make you aware. Aware of what matters most to you, aware of your boundaries and what you are willing to do—and not do—to make your life and work better. Awareness is the primary goal of coaching. When a client says, "I have never thought about that before," I know they are making progress. They are starting to become aware of how their actions played a role in getting them to the place they are now. They can also play a role in changing that place. What drives me nuts are clients that choose to see themselves as victims, meaning that they believe they have no choice. "This is just the way it is. There is nothing I can do about it." We can always do something.

This way of looking at your choices, feelings, and actions with curiosity, is awareness. I wonder why I did that? I wonder why that bothered me? There is no judgment – just awareness. I am a fan of journaling for this because it gets the judgment out of your head and on paper. Awareness about what your inner critic is saying is vital to letting it go. When you are aware of that negative chatter, you can ask yourself – is that true? Is it true I am not good enough? Is it true I am not qualified for that promotion? Most of the time, the answer is no, it is not true. We must acknowledge the chatter, question it and then we can let it go. What I don't want is for you to make decisions based on your inner negative thoughts.

Most of us spend time in neutral – just coasting through life and not paying attention to our reactions to it. My intention in writing this book is to get you to see that you have choices and opportunities to do things differently or more intentionally. We don't decide what happens to us. We do decide how we react. There is this nanosecond between an action and our response. A moment to decide how we want to show up and respond.

Taking control of your choices, your voice, and your actions is the way you start to live and lead by design. Look back over the work you did in this book and decide to act. Any action moves you forward. My clients get stuck. They internalize and overthink decisions. They see these decisions as huge and, in many cases, they are just decisions for right now. If you take this job or that one, you are just taking it for right now – not forever. When you feel stuck, take a deep breath, and do something.

My friend used to have this saying about dating. She

would call her date, "He'll do." He will do for tonight. I don't have to marry him, but I can go on a date with him. I think there are other areas in our lives that the answer may be, "That will do for now."

Self-Full

Self-care may seem selfish to some of you. It would have to me just a few years ago. Selflessness is seen as a noble thing. That really means no sense of self. How can that make you or anyone else happy? I like the expression – self-full. When you are full you have an excess of enthusiasm, energy and a sense of expansiveness to give more fully to the others in your life. Don't you know when you are present for your children? When you feel alive? The way to have more of that is to take the time to do the things that you have identified that fill you up and then do them! Just do them. It is not selfish to spend time on you. It allows you to be self-full.

Boundaries

If you say "Yes" to someone and you wanted to say "No," you are not honoring your boundaries. It is not that the person stepped over your boundaries, it is that you allowed them to do so. I know that I covered this already, but as you get to the end of this book, I want to leave you with clear boundaries. Think about what you will and won't allow in your life.

I don't work on Fridays. That is a boundary. When I take on a client or other obligation on a Friday, I get mad at myself. It is not their fault. It is mine. I moved the line. If we say that we don't answer emails after six and then answer one (I mean it is just one quick email, right?), you are saying that the boundary didn't matter. People believe what we do, not what we say. So, if you are serious put that in your email signature and don't answer emails after six. My publisher has an auto-response on her emails that say she is busy with clients and can't be reached until later. It is clearly a boundary that she has made for herself. I respect that. And I know as her client that when she is with me she is not answering any other emails. She is focused on me.

The easiest way to honor your boundaries is to let others know. If you want to have time to yourself every Saturday afternoon for two hours, tell your spouse and your children, and anyone else that asks for your time. It is easier if we are upfront about them. Be bold and say it out loud. We get to decide where and when to break a boundary. I am talking about it again because it is so important to choosing happy and living and leading by design.

Curiosity vs. Judgement

We make judgements every day. When someone pulls out in front of us in traffic, we judge that the person is a jerk or worse. When someone shows up late for a few days at work, we make a judgement that they are goofing off and need to be reprimanded. Our husband forgot our anniversary and we make a judgement that our anniversary doesn't matter, or worse, that we don't matter. We tend to believe our judgements. We even tell others about them. We make up stories to support our judgements. There is always another version.

Judgement is filling in the gaps, not questioning anything, focusing on the words or actions alone. Judgement is telling yourself a story without input from the one being judged. Curiosity is this moment of seeing the situation without the stories, meanings, or predictions. Curiosity is neutral; judgement is not. Curiosity is wondering if what you believe to be true could mean something else. And may not mean what you think it does!

Curiosity is—I wonder what is going on with that person that just pulled out in front of me? Why is that staff person running late lately? What is up with my husband that he missed my anniversary? When we are curious, we can ask questions to determine what the real story is. Not just the story we tell ourselves.

I am curious about what you have gotten from this experience. I am curious about what you are taking away that might allow you to live and lead by design and choose happy.

I hope what you have found is that you are Dorothy in the Wizard of Oz and realize that you always had the answer. You always knew what you needed and wanted. It is important that you listen and honor that. We don't need to reinvent ourselves into something better or some new polished version. Don't become the person you think you should be, just the version of you that is your essence. The best version.

We have looked at my Intentional Action Pillars—intuition, clarity, priority, and truth. We have examined how to live more intentionally. Choosing happy is your choice and within your grasp.

I am honored that you spent this time with me. My hope is that you found what you needed in this book.

"May you be happy.

May you be well.

May you be safe.

May you be peaceful and at ease."

—*Traditional Metta Meditation*

References

Acknowledgements

"All My Roads" (a song by Collin Raye)

How to Approach This Book

Williams, Margery, reissue edition, 1991. *Velveteen Rabbit.* Doubleday.

Dare to Choose Happy

McGraw, Dr. Philip C., 2003. *Self Matters: Creating Your Life from the Inside Out.* Free Press.

"How You Live (Turn Up the Music)" (a song by Point of Grace)

Intentional Action Pillars

Evans, Lynette. 2022. "Some say life begins at 40. Others at 50. All nonsense! Life begins when we decide to stop pleasing the audience. A simple view." Facebook, June 23, 2022. https://m.facebook.com/asimpleview/photos/a.458203054382365/1987966971405958/

Intuition—Use Your Inside Voice

"The power of vulnerability," a TED talk by Brené Brown posted in December 2010.

Edmondson, Amy C. and Chamorro-Premuzic, Thomas. "Today's Leaders Need Vulnerability, Not Bravado." *Harvard Business Review*, October 19, 2020.

Covey, Stephen R., 2020. *The 7 Habits Of Highly Effective People: Revised and Updated: 30th Anniversary Edition.* Simon & Schuster UK.

Clarity—The Missing Piece

Forleo, Marie, 2019. *Everything is Figureoutable.* Portfolio.

Hobby Lobby is the trademark of Hobby Lobby Stores, Inc.

Vision Board Kit for Women is manufactured by Bold Tuesday.

Laporte, Danielle, 2014. *The Fire Starter Sessions: A Soulful + Practical Guide to Creating Success on Your Own Terms.* Harmony.

Weatherly, Amy, "Tiny Buddha: Simple Wisdom for Complex Lives," https://tinybuddha.com/wisdom-quotes/

some-people-could-be-given-an-entire-field-of-roses-and-only-see-thorns-in-it/. 2023.

Practices-FeelingsSensations.pdf (hoffmaninstitute.org)

Priority—Getting the Right Things Done

Covey, Stephen R., 2020. *The 7 Habits Of Highly Effective People: Revised and Updated: 30th Anniversary Edition.* Simon & Schuster UK.

Mindful Practices, "Rocks, Pebbles and Sand: Prioritizing Your Life," Jun 15, 2020. YouTube video, 1:57. https://youtu.be/cPgMeKfQFq8.

Bungay Stanier, Michael. 2010. *Do More Great Work: Stop the Busywork. Start the Work That Matters.* Workman Publishing Company.

Hyatt, Michael, 2019. *Free to Focus: A Total Productivity System to Achieve More by Doing Less.* Baker Books.

Kondo, Marie, 2014. *The Life-Changing Magic of Tidying Up: The Japanese Art of Decluttering and Organizing.* Ten Speed Press.

Goodwill is the trademark of GOODWILL INDUSTRIES INTERNATIONAL, INC.

UPS is the trademark of UNITED PARCEL SERVICE OF AMERICA, INC.

SaneBox is the trademark of SANEBOX, INC.

Microsoft Outlook is the trademark of Microsoft Corporation.

Notion is the trademark of Notion Labs, Inc.

Acree, Jules. https://julesacree.com/.

reMarkable 2 is manufactured by reMarkable®

Medlock, Kimberly, 2015. *Smarter Work Habits that Matter.* KWM Publishing.

Chicos is manufactured by CHICO'S DISTRIBUTION SERVICES, LLC.

J. Jill is the trademark of J. Jill Acquisition LLC.

Duhigg, Charles, 2012. *The Power of Habit: Why We Do What We Do, and How to Change.* Cornerstone Digital.

Sejdiu, Guxim, 2021. Positive Quotes FaceBook group. Facebook, October 13, 2021. https://www.facebook.com/photo/?fbid=4368006429961690&set=g.1558558054440380.

Truth—Speak Your Truth Even When Your Voice Trembles

Maya Angelou, "Quotable Quote," Goodreads. https://www.goodreads.com/quotes/706432-each-time-a-woman-stands-up-for-herself-without-knowing

Patterson, Kerry, Grenny, Joseph, McMillan, Ron, and Switzer, Al, 2011. *Crucial Conversations Tools for Talking When Stakes Are High, Second Edition.* McGraw Hill, Second Edition.

Scott, Susan, 2004. *Fierce Conversations: Achieving Success at Work and in Life One Conversation at a Time.* Berkely, Reprint Edition.

Lichtenstein PhD, Marsha, 2019. *Perfect Pitch: How to Speak Up for Yourself in Everyday Relationships.* Smart Cookie Books.

The Wirdz Daily Motivational Quotes Facebook group, 2021. Facebook, March 24, 2021. https://www.facebook.com/thewirdz/photos/you-cant-keep-getting-mad-at-people-for-sucking-the-life-out-of-you-if-you-keep-/2819410848270610/

Leading By Design

Baum, L. Frank. 2010. *The Wonderful Wizard of Oz.* Oxford World's Classics. London, England: Oxford University Press.

Sockolov, Matthew. "Loving Kindness Meditation—Cultivating an Open Heart." One Mind Dharma. August 10, 2018. https://oneminddharma.com/loving-kindness-meditation/

About the Author

Darienne Mobley, PCC

As a life and leadership coach, speaker, and trainer, Darienne Mobley empowers individuals and teams to be their best. She accelerates change for her clients, providing guidance with navigating difficult work-related relationships, solving problems, and offering alternative perspectives that clients may not be able to see, so they can become better and healthier leaders.

With the inner aspects of personal development, she guides her clients to further develop self-trust, to become more confident in who they are and the value they offer, along with gaining confidence with everyday decisions and increased clarity about their future goals.

With 35 years of experience in the tourism industry, Darienne had the distinct honor of serving as the Director of Tourism for Mississippi and Louisiana, working at the highest levels of state government and many positions in between. She utilizes the skills and experience she gained through her tourism experience to guide her clients. Darienne earned her Professional Coach Certification designation with the International Coaching Federation. Her intention is always the same: to help her clients do life and work better.

Supporting women leaders is Darienne's sweet spot. As they say, "we teach what we know best"—and Darienne is a woman leader who knows the issues that women leaders face. When we are pulled in so many directions and do not believe we are showing up in any area of our lives as well as we should, we are our own worst enemies. We also believe (is this a Southern thing?) that we must take care of everybody else before we get to take care of ourselves. Darienne is committed to help women change that paradigm. Working with Darienne is a game changer. Not only does she work with clients one-to-one, she also coaches with groups as well as retreats.

One of Darienne's most popular programs is her "Dare to Lead and Live with Intention" group coaching program. She takes eight women on a five-month journey to explore living with intention, purpose and clarity. You will connect with other women who are right where you are and get private coaching with Darienne as well as the group experience.

Visit Darienneinc.com to see options to see how she might benefit you. Setting up a complimentary call is the first step.

CPSIA information can be obtained
at www.ICGtesting.com
Printed in the USA
JSHW042053030523
41185JS00006B/23